T0272514

The Deep-Rooted Marriage

The
Deep-Rooted
Marriage

Cultivating Intimacy, Healing, and Delight

Dan B. Allender, PhD
AND Steve Call, PhD

W PUBLISHING GROUP

AN IMPRINT OF THOMAS NELSON

The Deep-Rooted Marriage

Copyright © 2025 Dr. Dan B. Allender and Dr. Steve Call

All rights reserved. No portion of this book may be reproduced, stored in a retrieval system, or transmitted in any form or by any means—electronic, mechanical, photocopy, recording, scanning, or other—except for brief quotations in critical reviews or articles, without the prior written permission of the publisher.

Published in Nashville, Tennessee, by W Publishing, an imprint of Thomas Nelson.

Published in association with Yates & Yates, www.yates2.com.

Thomas Nelson titles may be purchased in bulk for educational, business, fundraising, or sales promotional use. For information, please email SpecialMarkets@ ThomasNelson.com.

Unless otherwise noted, Scripture quotations are taken from The Holy Bible, New International Version®, NIV®. Copyright © 1973, 1978, 1984, 2011 by Biblica, Inc.® Used by permission of Zondervan. All rights reserved worldwide. www.zondervan.com. The "NIV" and "New International Version" are trademarks registered in the United States Patent and Trademark Office by Biblica, Inc.®

Scripture quotations marked NLT are taken from the Holy Bible, New Living Translation. © 1996, 2004, 2015 by Tyndale House Foundation. Used by permission of Tyndale House Publishers, Inc., Carol Stream, Illinois 60188. All rights reserved.

Names and identifying characteristics of some individuals have been changed to preserve their privacy.

Any internet addresses, phone numbers, or company or product information printed in this book are offered as a resource and are not intended in any way to be or to imply an endorsement by Thomas Nelson, nor does Thomas Nelson vouch for the existence, content, or services of these sites, phone numbers, companies, or products beyond the life of this book.

ISBN 978-1-4003-4459-8 (audiobook)
ISBN 978-1-4003-4458-1 (ePub)
ISBN 978-1-4003-4726-1 (ITPE)
ISBN 978-1-4003-4446-8 (HC)

Library of Congress Control Number: 2024938947

Printed in the United States of America

24 25 26 27 28 LBC 5 4 3 2 1

To Rebecca Anne Allender
"In all the world, there is no heart for me like yours. In all the world, there is no love for you like mine." (Maya Angelou)
—Dan

To my dear wife, Lisa
It is a privilege to walk this path with you. You are truly a gift.
—Steve

Contents

CONTENTS

PART 3: GENERATING GOODNESS BETWEEN
YOU AND BEYOND YOU

A Note from Dan

It was one of those nights I couldn't sleep.

I turned over and gazed at the lump of covers I knew was my wife. For some reason I needed to be sure she was breathing. There was no health issue in mind; I just had to know for sure. Eventually, her subtle, quiet breathing quelled my concern, and I tried to fall back asleep.

Memories started to crawl into the bed and nudged me to acknowledge their presence. I elbowed one or two to let them know I had no interest, but they persisted. I finally submitted to being fully conscious, and the memory of our second night as a married couple rose to the surface.

We were twentysomethings sitting in a car on a steep, snowy road, unable to get up a North Carolina mountain and reach a little cabin that would serve as a honeymoon suite. It was our destination because it was free. We were as poor as proverbial church mice, and we had at that moment just enough money to get back home to Florida. We certainly did not have the means to pay for a tow service or a hotel.

Less than forty-eight hours into our marriage, and we were in a jam, facing our first challenge as husband and wife.

I wonder, how long was it for you and your partner?

However many hours or days in, and whatever the struggle, there was a first time you were in a tight spot with your spouse. A position where it was plausible to think, *This moment is hard. But it can be the making of us.*

And there have been countless more moments like it since.

Every marriage is an ongoing story with highs and lows, joys and disasters. And it is shaping each of us, for better or worse.

No one, not one single human being, wants to be shaped by their marriage for worse, but it happens. So, of course, the questions are, *How do we avoid that? How can we build a stronger, healthier marriage, one that shapes us for the better?*

Steve, my longtime colleague and friend, and I have been in dialogue with couples about this topic for decades. Between the two of us, we have more than seventy years of therapeutic experience involving hundreds of marriages. This book is a culmination of our longtime dream to distill and synthesize our most critical observations, insights, and suggestions.

We are psychologists, therapists, professors, and, most importantly, spouses just like you. We've not only led others in building stronger marriages but also fumbled through our own personal growth. Steve has journeyed with Lisa, and I have walked with Becky.

Most couples want a better marriage, but the risk and work it would require seem insurmountable. They've made efforts to stoke the flame and renew the early sweetness and wonder, perhaps achieving it on a special trip, only to feel it slip away once the mundane and demanding realities of work and children crowd back in.

Many good marriage books offer advice about how to spice up your marriage. This is not one of them.

Steve and I start from a different premise: we are heading to a banquet of delight, as promised in Psalm 23, and along the way, we will walk through some dark valleys. The hard moments and the suffering are an inescapable part of our journey toward connection and closeness. Some of us will rage at the darkness. Others will withdraw. Still others will press through with brute force but gain no new awareness, growth, or intimacy.

Steve and I want to point you to another path, one that human instinct and societal voices will not lead you to.

Our culture looks to the future and pushes forward with a relentless insistence that not much can be learned from the past other than the need to do better. What we lose in this narrow view, though, is what made us who we are today.

Every marriage is a story of two people formed by different worlds joining together to create a universe that has never existed before. Your marriage is unique in all its goodness and in all that needs redemption.

Steve and I will explore with you how you came to be together and formed the new universe of your marriage. What heartache and hope, what trauma and dreams (often unaddressed and unseen) shaped the expectations and demands you now direct toward your partner and yourself?

Understanding the past allows us to make sense of what's not working in the present. If we don't explore our earlier stories, we won't grasp how our histories of brokenness and beauty are playing out now. And we'll be bound to repeat them in one form or another.

In a state of unawareness, we'll continue making efforts, but not in ways that lead to change. "Just trying harder" will keep us stuck in ingrained patterns that cause disconnection, and eventually we will conclude that change is not possible.

Not engaging our stories is like cutting off the top of a weed instead of yanking it out by its roots. If we consider our marriages to be young trees we hope will grow and flourish, those weed roots will keep crowding our tree roots until we do something about them.

Once we yank out the weed roots, our tree roots will get the nutrients they need. Our tree will receive life and strength.

If we tend to the roots, good fruit will grow.

The weed roots Steve and I are inviting you to address are the ways, means, and consequences of past heartache and trauma. You were formed in your earliest classroom, by your family of origin, in many ways you're unaware of. If you don't look deeply below the surface and see why you *function* the way you do and why you *feel* the way you do, you'll be letting those weed roots keep you from change. Healing. Newness. Deeper intimacy. More delight.

The hurts that shaped you may have been subtle and easy to overlook. But often what is common or "normal" remains like a small stone in your shoe. While it is not fatal, it compromises your capacity to walk well. And some hurts are not at all subtle or easy to overlook, and we need to see if we can invite more healing into those deepest places.

Know that Steve and I are not inviting you to a blaming mentality—only honest reflection on how you came to be who you are, how you might be formed in new ways, and how you could write a new story with your spouse.

Your marriage is where redemption is meant to grow. God intends for it to be not merely good or happy, but transformative. You will become who your marriage exposes and invites you to be. This is a far richer and more compelling vision of marriage than only getting along or resolving conflict through compromise. You are either becoming more like Jesus together and because of each other, or you are not.

For some, the mention of God, or Jesus, or any religious connotation is a no-go, an offense or turnoff. And no wonder. What many religious people have made of marriage is a fetish, or worse, an unequal bondage of rules and roles rather than what God invites—a wild faith journey into the hope of transformation. If you are not particularly religious, give us a shot, and see where it takes you.

Throughout this journey you will hear from Steve and me, and a bit from our wives, Lisa and Becky. We will share the good, bad, and ugly of our marriages—although, as we say in chapter 2, this is not a marriage memoir. We don't presume our marriages are like yours or are a model for what to do; we offer them as examples of how it can look. We all are different, but over the years Steve and I have seen commonalities across couples—the typical problems and processes for growing strong roots and good fruit. It is our desire to walk with you through this orchard and lead you to taste some sweet fruit.

This "walk," of course, does not involve you simply reading these pages, but using them as a map as you step through the terrain.

It will involve moments of coming to your partner with more curiosity and patience, seeing more in them than you ever have before, and being struck by the tremendous gift they are to you.

If you're anything like me, it might mean looking at your slumbering spouse, feeling deeply grateful they are beside you, and wondering what life would be like if suddenly they were not.

I think again of that night of sleeplessness, when I needed to be soothed by watching Becky breathe. I needed to be reminded she was alive, I suppose, because I know one day she won't be, and I might still be here. Instead of seeing her bright eyes looking into mine, I'd have only memories and the anticipation of seeing her again in a far more beautiful place.

I may one day be alone on a snowy North Carolina mountain trying to figure out how to make it home. No one would share a decades-old memory with me in the way that clump of covers could. She knows, like I do, how we caught a ride with kind strangers who took us to our cabin on that snowy mountain road. We eventually found our way to a place of strength and peace together.

There are calamities we all face that are far more difficult than being stuck on a snowy mountain road, and there are moments we feel far from our partners. How can we find our way back to each other and a path through the hard seasons?

And will that be the question we come back to when we're feeling hurt or confused, frustrated or worn out?

Life is indeed short, brutal, and stunningly beautiful. Coming to learn this at increasingly deeper levels has led me to this resolve: I will not let my brief days pass without attending to the person most important to me, who God uniquely designed, who God continually uses to trouble and arouse me to the wonder of redemption.

To some degree, we all are on that snowy mountain road waiting for rescue, knowing a shared struggle, having to choose whether we'll lean toward each other or away. If the process of making your way back "home" together while growing closer feels like a pilgrimage you want to make, come walk with us. We'd be honored to join you and offer what we have learned.

Part One

Getting Clear-Eyed About Who You Are

Falling into Each Other's Arms

Dan

To love is . . . good, for love is difficult. For one human
being to love another is perhaps the most difficult task
of all, the epitome, the ultimate test. It is that striving
for which all other striving is merely preparation.

RAINER MARIA RILKE

Every marriage is a tapestry. The threads of a vertical life interlace with a horizontal life, forming a stunning picture on one side and rough knots on the other. Both people are beautiful, because they were made in the image of God. They both are also broken and flawed due to their traumatic ancestry and natural proclivity to sin. They each are a glorious mess as individuals and even more dramatic and compelling as a couple.

It is in this place of intimacy that both our imperfect and exquisite qualities are most visible. No one knows more about my brokenness than my wife, Becky, and no one has seen me at my best like she has. The same is likely true for you and your spouse. We all are meant for this—to know and be known—and it is in marriage that we can see into the kaleidoscope of our complex identities most clearly. The deepest closeness provides exclusive access to our deepest places.

As we open ourselves to our spouses, we also can open ourselves to the heart of God, allowing his extravagant grace, compassion, and delight to trickle down into the core of us. It is, in fact, part of why he brought us together, so we could know intimacy with each other and with him—and experience his love in profound and powerful ways.

Whatever your relational dynamic is today, whether it is on the rocks, soaring above the clouds, or living somewhere in the middle orbit of reality, I want you to know: *you and your partner are meant for more.* No matter how difficult or sweet your marriage is, God created you for more than whatever you are experiencing today.

We are here not just to survive or even have a "good" marriage. Every marriage is meant to be a taste of heaven, a glimpse back into Eden, and an anticipation of what will one day be true. We are the face of God to each other.

In our partners' moments of vulnerability and failure, we reveal God's kindness and patience to them. In their fear and pain, we channel his strength and comfort. As we have the honor of seeing who they are up close, we express God's sheer adoration and enjoyment of his creation.

Of course, we often fail to do this. Many times, sadly, I have been for Becky a taste of hell, and, likewise, she has been an acrid presence for me. This is not because we don't love each other or belong together; it is because we possess frailties no human can escape. But it is by design that these rise to the surface in marriage, so we can sense how God treats our hurts and needs, and so he can grab hold of broken parts of us and make us new.

No matter the ups and downs, we are meant to be the presence of God that brings transformation, doing so in a way no one else possibly could.

To put it bluntly, we are meant to drive each other crazy, and welcome each other to sanity, wholeness, and joy.

If this is the case, why isn't everyone experiencing this?

No one will ever experience what is possible if they fail to engage what is true. We are beautiful and we are broken; we need to embrace both realities about ourselves and our spouses, and especially during conflict. In those difficult moments we have the potential not only to *taste the more*, but to *become the more* we are meant to be.

Hand-on-the-Heart Talk

Our family became a ski family because my publisher once offered an incredible perk for signing a book contract: a family season pass to ski at four resorts in Summit County, Colorado. At the time, I had only skied once, and our children had never buckled up on a slope. Becky was our sole elegant skier. Because it was free, no matter if we hated it, we were going to become a ski family.

When we began, our three-year-old son, Andrew, took to the mountain like a duck to water. He was swift, sure, and, like his mother, elegant. On his first day on the slope, he ran his first black run. A black run is the most challenging and often most dangerous slope—steep and with no grooming to make the slope easily traversed. When he was eight, he had a serious fall that we feared would kill him. He survived, but for a year he was hesitant and timid on his skis.

The next year, we went skiing around Thanksgiving, when there was little snow and lots of hard-packed ice. We came to a blue run (which is a slope that is comfortable for intermediate skiers), icy and cold, and our girls asked Becky and me if they could go in for an early lunch. We agreed, and they skied off, leaving Becky, Andrew, and me looking down at a formidable but skiable slope.

Andrew began to whine, and Becky solicitously affirmed him and encouraged him to try. It didn't work.

After a few minutes I stepped in and gruffly told him to get ready to go, because we were all cold, hungry, and miserable.

His fear and defiance rose, as did my irritation and verbiage.

Becky finally intervened and asked me, "Why don't you ski down and wait for us, and I'll stay with him until he is ready?"

I complied, with reservation. If she wanted to manage his fear, good for her. But I doubted it was the right approach.

I skied down and waited. And waited. Forever. I could see Becky two hundred yards up the hill, talking to and encouraging Andrew, but eventually this resulted in him sitting down and trying to kick off his skis.

I waited until I could bear it no more, and then I began the long, arduous march up the side of the mountain to motivate and retrieve my son, propping my skis and poles on my shoulder. I was furious. After forty yards of slipping and sliding, I finally went to the edge of the slope where there was enough snow to hold my boots without slipping, and it was an exhausting trudge. Each step I became colder in heart and overheated in body.

Once I arrived at the top, I put my skis on and began to move toward Becky and Andrew. I saw Becky ease from his side as she glided to stand between us; I would have to encounter her before I could get to him. She could sense I was convinced that Andrew needed a firmer influence.

Twenty yards away from her, I mouthed the word *move*.

She quietly and tenderly shook her head. *No.*

I glided closer, now inches away, and said coldly and quietly, "Move."

What she did next, to this day, decades later, makes my head spin.

She put her hand on my heart and said, "I know the men who have brought you heartache and humiliated you. I know what it has cost you. And I know that is not what you want to do to your son."

I don't know why my heart softened then and not during a hundred times of other failures, but I began to cry. What I expected was my wife's defensive anger to protect our son from his angry father. Instead,

I experienced the flashing images of a coach, a mentor, my father, and the other men who had humiliated me. In one of the swiftest and most elegant jujitsu moments of my life, my wife took my legs out from under me, and tears flooded my face with memories and the horror of what I had been about to do to my son. Far from a shaming attack, it was the jolt I needed to see the reality I was barreling into.

What happened next, I can barely write without weeping.

Becky saw my tears, and her hand pushed slightly harder against my heart. She looked further into my eyes and said, "You are a good man."

She saw my humanness, both the brokenness and beauty, and met me with empathy, love, and belief. With a physical touch, she reminded me of our intimacy and trust, and signaled that she knew and was reaching a deep part of me. Then she addressed my wounds from the past, my struggle in the present, and my yearning for a healthy, joyful future. It was, altogether, a reassurance to me that I was seen—and that I could *become more*. It was a taste of heaven, loving me and pulling me toward goodness, and precisely what my soul needed.

After Becky delivered those dumbfounding words, she disappeared down the slope, leaving me with my terrified son, who was still sprawled on the ground.

I dropped down beside him, lifted him onto my lap, and wrapped my arm around him.

I acknowledged the immense bravery of his mother. I confessed my anger. And I told him how sad I was to have scared him.

He looked me square in my face and put his hand on my heart, just as his mother had. "Mom is right, Dad," he said. "You are a good man, but too often angry."

I didn't know whether to weep, laugh, or hug him.

I have never in this lifetime received a greater honor or accolade than I did that day. A thousand statements from other people have seared me over these seven decades, but no words have settled into my soul as a solace and strength as much as those blessings from my wife and son.

We got off the ground, awkwardly. I set out a tentative plan about how he could make his way down, and he concurred. After a few deep breaths, he turned his skis downhill and began the journey. After twenty yards, he hit a blue patch of ice and started to skid out of control, and I saw him head for the edge where there was deeper snow and a cliff. I held my breath, and, once he got to the edge, I saw him take his first deep powder turn. Next, with amazement, I saw him glide to greet his mom with a huge hug.

I took in the glory with a sigh and smile, and then set off. I made three or four turns and, out of nowhere, found myself in the air, almost parallel to the ground with my arms out like wings. Apparently, I had crossed my tips and flown face forward. For a fleeting moment, airborne, I felt like a bird. A dodo bird. Gravity took its toll, and I hit the ground first with my chest and face.

The explosion at impact was intense. My skis scattered, and one glove and pole flew off, while the other remained on my wrist. I rose again and spiraled in the air until I rolled another forty yards in a desecrated ball. I came to a stop and, eventually, my breath caught up with me, and I began to gasp. It took minutes for me to rise and begin to collect the yard-sale debris scattered around the slope.

I glanced at Andrew and Becky, who looked horrified and concerned.

Once I was glued back together, I skied down, and, as I arrived, they turned to each other, hugged, and fell into a heap, unable to contain their laughter. Now that they knew I was alive and ambulatory, their fear melted into hilarity. The tension of that time plus the acrobatic brilliance of my flight took them over the edge. I watched, slightly irritated, but also aware there was laughter in heaven as well.

What could have been a humiliating, disastrous interaction with my son and an equally dangerous fall was not only averted, but was also met with laughter. Eventually, they rose, and both reached out to pull me into their embrace, and we wept, laughed, and shivered together until it was time to descend.

Andrew raced ahead. Becky and I hung back for a few seconds, and, before we pushed off, she told me, "You will never forget this moment, and you will never be the same."

Without a doubt, she was right.

I am not the same man who coldly raged up the side of that mountain. In those gutting moments, the Spirit of God softened my heart and awakened in me a longing for gentleness and humility. I wanted him to generate more of that in me, to change my automatic relational reactions. Over time, as more moments of friction and grace played out between Becky and me, and I responded to the Spirit's nudging, my heart and my style of relating changed dramatically.

I am, of course, nowhere near perfect. I am grieved to confess that since then, at times I've forgotten those moments and failed my son and many others. But I did *progress*, I did *transform*, and so, just as Becky said, I am not the same man I was that day.

And she and I do not have the same marriage.

An Atmosphere of Transformation and Intimacy

Becky and I have become more aware of tender areas to treat with care and of broken tendencies to redirect. After addressing them together for years, we don't feel caught in the relational patterns we developed when we were younger; we notice when they creep in and work to gently steer out of them.

We've become quicker to speak compassion and grace when we stumble. To receive truth and gentleness when we feel vulnerable. To free and empower each other when we feel stuck. Divisive moments have become less frequent and are resolved more quickly, which has not only brought relief, but also left room for more joyful, fulfilling connection.

All told, little by little, we've allowed ourselves to be seen and known and reached by the other in increasingly deeper ways, generating a kind of goodness and sweet intimacy that leaves us in awe. After forty-seven years of marriage, I am still discovering new ways Becky is lovely, staggering, and amazing. I am continually moved by simply beholding her and often find myself thinking, with a sense of wonder, *I can't believe I am married to you.*

We have not "arrived." We still have conflicts, hurts, tension; we are still human. But we are so much further along than we were. We are more in tune with ourselves and each other, with how God's love and life can reshape, reassure, and renew us. And, year after year, we are surprised by the ways God keeps letting us *taste the more* and *become the more* we are meant to be, together.

Past, Present, and Future

My wife on that Colorado slope was brilliant, courageous, and tender. She was up against a man whose anger and verbosity had saved him from the maw of a mentally ill mother, and she did not back down. She fought for our good in a gracious yet resolute way.

For me to receive what Becky offered, I had to refuse to do what I had done a million times in the past to keep my mother at bay—*intimidate.* What Becky had to do, in an instant, was what she had seldom done in her own past—*stand her ground.* For her to stand in my way, speak, and call forth the better angels of my heart required her to do what had been too dangerous to do as a child with her belittling, antagonistic mother.

Over a series of countless events in our childhoods, we all developed relational patterns that enabled us to survive whatever pain we continually encountered. As adults, we instinctively live out those same patterns in the present. If we want a redeemed future and a more beautiful marriage, we must excavate and sift through what shaped us in the past. For most of us, this will feel either too dangerous or superfluous. Why mess with the forgotten past when we have real issues we need to resolve in the present?[1]

We can see the answer in a picture of gardening. If you want a flourishing garden, you need to tend to the soil, even bring in manure. You must tend to the dirt and get nutrients to the roots. If you are dealing with weeds, it is not enough to cut them off at the top and hope they go away. You have to dig down deep into the soil to extract the roots and kill what will diminish your crop. It is messy, dirty work, but the result of good care and wisdom is delicious, nourishing fruit.

The same will be true for your marriage. You must dig down into your story, and reach the cause of whatever you're seeing at the surface level now. You must understand the past if you want to change the present.

Turning back to the marriage tapestry, if you and your spouse are willing, you will bring your past threads, both beautiful and stained, and together weave a glory that, if seen from the vantage point of eternity, reflects the incomprehensible beauty of God. While no one is perfect and no marriage is without flaws, every marriage can defy the past, redeem the present, and thrive in the future.

Start Dreaming

Marriage is a wild, at times terrifying, journey into the fullness of what love, with honesty and humility, can bring to this earth. Your marriage is meant to transform, redeem, and free you to be fully alive.

For many of us, this is an audacious view. But even if it feels like a considerable stretch, let's explore it: If you let yourself believe this, what could this mean for your relationship?

How might God weave more beauty into your marriage, create something new in your heart, bring a bit of heaven into your dynamic?

Maybe he could guide you into healthier relational patterns, ones that lead to more love and truth, not division and resentment. He might help you each feel more known and delighted in, held up and believed in, even at your lowest points. Perhaps conflicts that were once roadblocks to intimacy and transformation could become glass doors you can see through, open, and move through—something you can understand and navigate together.

Wherever your imagination wanders, dare to ask, *What do I dream for my partner and me? How would I love to see our story unfold in the years to come? How might we step into transformation, freedom, and vibrancy?*

Also explore: Who do I want to become? Who would I like to be in moments of tension with my partner? What would a more curious, honest, compassionate, and patient version of me look like?

As someone who sits with couples who are living out all kinds of stories, I am "sitting" with you now. Whatever story you find yourself in today, I join you, wondering with you how you could be the face of God to your spouse.

I wonder how your spouse could be the face of God to you.

And I wonder how he might astonish you both with *the more* he will bring you into, if you let him.

two

Following the Tracks of Love

*I fell in love with her courage, her sincerity, and her flaming
self-respect. And it's these things I'd believe in, even if the
whole world indulged in wild suspicions that she wasn't all
she should be. I love her and it is the beginning of everything.*

F. SCOTT FITZGERALD

W hy are you looking at me that way?" Becky asked, acting like I had
done something odd or irreverent.

"What? What have I done? What do you mean?" I replied reflexively.

"You're staring at me, and it feels weird," she explained. "What's
going on?"

I had been in a daze, unaware that I'd been staring, time traveling to
a December moment when she and I were twenty-three. The soft snow of
an Ohio winter was quietly falling, and I was walking with the woman I
hoped, truly hoped, would one day be troubled enough to marry me. She
was wearing white corduroys with a mustard-colored felted wool sweater

and red clogs. Her voice was as soft as the snow, her hand held mine, and I wanted the walk to last for eternity.

In the present moment, Becky was wearing a nearly identical outfit, and, even though we were almost fifty years from that December moment, it felt as real to me now as it did then.

Why did she marry a seminarian who barely believed in God, a troubled man who was alternately angry and grieving over his own failures? What could possibly have enabled her to take one of the biggest risks of a lifetime and bind her heart to mine? Why I married her is clearer to me today than it was five decades ago, because back then I'd only been able to say that I was in love. Much reflection from a distance has brought about some insight.

Before I explain more and share how Becky's and my stories collided, I want to assure you that you have not stumbled into a memoir. This book is ultimately about you and your spouse and how you can move toward experiencing deeper intimacy. The first way Steve and I want to help you do that is through building awareness of your story—how you came together, what happened before then, what happened after. With that awareness, you will be able to see where you can grow, heal, and transform in ways that bring you closer.

In this chapter, I want to provide you with a landscape, a sense of context, for our coming discussions about your experiences and to "go first," showing you how you might start to reflect as we continue.

We begin by reflecting because it is nearly impossible to go forward until we go back—until we understand why we married each other. It holds the key to our beauty as couples and gives a window into our brokenness.

A Life-Changing Trip to Pluto

I was a college freshman escaping the Ohio chill over spring break, living my best life in sunny Fort Lauderdale. And, like many eighteen-year-olds in 1970, my "best life" involved a few illicit activities.

Holding a thick envelope with ten thousand dollars in cash inside, I strolled out of a condo and onto the beach, hoping to avoid getting busted. I closely watched my surroundings for several minutes, but no one appeared except a beautiful young woman, and I had a sense that I knew her.

I flashed back to my tenth-grade French class, when I'd drop my pencil to gaze at her magnificent legs. I'd also occasionally maneuver to leave class when she did, so I could engage her in conversation using a Brooklyn accent—unusual, yes, but no doubt very charming. Yet I'd made no more impression on her than a passing irregular French verb.

On the beach, I followed her and called her name, "Becky! Becky!" She turned and didn't seem to recognize me, so I told her my name, and we embraced slightly. We talked for a few minutes; she also was attending college in Ohio and spending spring break in Florida. I asked if she wanted to join me and some friends at a hotel nearby. She knew a few of them from high school, and she agreed.

The group of us spent the afternoon frolicking on the beach and talking in the hotel. When we all dug into delivered pizza a few hours later, I saw one of my college friends sitting closer and closer to Becky; he was obviously hitting on her. I could have easily pounded his face into a pepperoni pizza, but it didn't seem a wise way to impress Becky.

Somehow or other, I had to get her away from this vagabond. I sidled up to her and asked, "Would you have any interest in taking a rocket ship to Pluto?" At the time, it seemed a reasonable request, given that I was somewhat under the influence of hallucinogens and Becky was sipping a beer.

To my utter shock, she said yes and began to collect a bedspread, ice buckets for helmets, and straws as a mechanism for oxygen far up in the breathless atmosphere.

The evening was magical. I narrated a thousand moments on our trip into space, which, thrillingly, stretched out to four hours. After we landed on earth, I got her phone number and hotel name so I could contact her the next day.

When I came to my senses the next afternoon, however, tragedy struck: *I could not find her number.* I was crestfallen, at a loss.

All I could do was party on.

The morning I left for the airport, I dropped psilocybin (some hallucinogenic mushrooms) and took a cab to check in. I gave my bag to the airport handler at the curb, telling him I was going to Columbus, Ohio, and walked inside to validate my ticket. The ticket agent took one look at it and said, "Sorry kid, this is a one-way ticket from Columbus, Ohio, to Fort Lauderdale."

I freaked. Somewhere along the way, I must have picked up someone else's ticket and left mine in my luggage, which was now headed to Columbus without me. I also had put ninety-five hundred dollars in that now-unreachable luggage and had only a five-dollar bill in my pocket.

I could barely think, I was so panicked. I did what any low-level, middle-class drug dealer would do: I called my mother.

As I have hinted, my mother was a deeply disturbed, erratic, unpredictable, mentally ill woman who could have easily been diagnosed with borderline personality disorder. We had a volatile and highly enmeshed relationship, but I could never have predicted what she did that day.

Hearing my plight, she said, "You got yourself into this mess, you get yourself out," then hung up on me.

Stunned, I started grasping for other options. I remembered that Becky also had been planning to leave that day—to drive back to Ohio with her friends—and she'd been staying at a hotel called The Beach . . . *something*, I couldn't remember the last word. So, in desperation, I exchanged my five-dollar bill for a pocketful of dimes, got a phone book, and started calling every hotel that began with *The Beach*, asking for a Becky Gilbert.

Five dimes in, I realized the room might not be under her name, so I started asking each hotel employee if there were four girls from Ohio there. Each time I heard, "No Becky Gilbert," and "How am I supposed to know where the girls are from?" along with a slam of the phone. Then I remembered that Becky and her friends had been driving a white Datsun, so I added that to my other two questions.

After making a total of thirty calls, I'd gotten thirty hang-ups. On my thirty-first call, I went through the three questions and was about to get another hang-up, when the person said, "Wait a minute, there's a white Datsun leaving the parking lot now."

I begged him to stop the car and ask for a Becky Gilbert.

After a few minutes, I heard the sweetest female voice in the universe say, "Hi, this is Becky. Who is asking for me?"

Becky and her friends agreed to let me join their road trip to Ohio on the condition that I did all the driving—seventeen hours over a thousand miles. I was elated.

Many hours into the trip, there was an incident at a gas station in Georgia. When I went into the store to pay, a few guys started hassling me. After one of them pushed me, I decked him, and by the enraged look of his friends, I knew I needed to get out fast. As I ran out of the gas station, I spied an open and unattended cash register. Since I was already in trouble and dead broke, I grabbed a few twenties on my way out.

Unfortunately, I soon discovered these guys were prone to holding a grudge.

I jumped back into the Datsun, where the girls had been waiting, and floored it. As we sped away from the gas station, three cars started following us with shotguns. They shot at our tires, mainly to scare us and make us feel their fury, it seemed, but there were indeed bullets flying our direction. I did the only thing I could—I kept pressing that little Datsun to its limits—and eventually they gave up the pursuit.

I then drove us all the way back to Ohio, and we never spoke of the interaction at the gas station.

Two things can be summarized from these encounters: (1) Becky had enough data to rightfully flee from me for the remainder of her life, and (2) I fell madly in love with her in all her wildness, kindness, unpredictability, and beauty.

Alas, we parted ways and didn't speak again for five years, and the story of our reuniting is exponentially weirder than this one.

Suffice to say, eventually something brought us together again. From an accurate and enduring perspective, God brought us together. But seldom does God intervene like a *deus ex machina*, snatch us out of our plight, plunk us down, and say, "Marry that one." So, it is also accurate to say that things in our past drew Becky and me together—and the same can be said for you and your spouse.

Below the Surface of Every Story

Every marriage is built on the unconscious intention to find redemption. We look at the extraordinary person we're dating and, somehow, in our bones we sense, *You will give me what I never had before. You will give my body and heart what I know I need.* We typically are unaware of this impulse. And of our unmet needs. And of how the other might rescue us.

When I married Becky at age twenty-three, I had no idea I was troubled or difficult. I had no idea what she brought to my life other than laughter, kindness, and arousal. I considered our origin story to be simply confirmation of God's goodness and our love. If you had asked me, "Did you marry Becky to redeem the heartache and brokenness of your past? Did you find her irresistible because she saved you from your mother?" I would have thought you were crazy and stupid. I wouldn't have the same reaction today.

The story of Fort Lauderdale holds a few indicators of why we married: Becky could willingly "fly to Pluto," be captured by a storyteller, and bear getting shot at without needing to debrief. At first blush, this all seems absurd. The only way to make sense of it—or of how any of us fit with our partners—is to look at the soil in which our roots grew.

I am an only child born from a marriage that was tragically broken. My mother was wickedly insecure, flighty, helpless, mean, hilarious, and desperate for care. My father, who died in a car accident when I was four, had been addicted to morphine and engaged in multiple affairs. My mom needed me to give meaning and passion to her empty, broken life.

When she remarried, she chose a kind, passive, dutiful man, the antithesis of my biological father. He suffered much of her craziness but had no clue how to handle her peculiarities or periodic suicidal, homicidal moods. He left that for me to manage, even when I was a young child. I often did so by staying incredibly dialed in to her emotional state and distracting her with soothing, compelling stories. This became my job, my role in life. I learned to constantly read my mother and keep her insanity at bay through gathering and telling stories.

As you can imagine, my mother's extreme neediness wore on me, so I also learned to keep her from smothering me by causing trouble. I was her all in all, until I did something crazy or dangerous. If I rode my bike into a car, she would cut me off for a few days. If I got caught blowing up a mailbox with an M-80, I might be sent to the coldest regions of Siberia, where she wouldn't talk to me for days. Receiving emotional space from my mom was my version of going on a resort vacation.

Becky, on the other hand, was the middle child of a father who experienced severe highs and lows and was eccentric, unpredictable, and hilarious, at least when he was manic. When he was depressed, he looked to Becky to brighten his despair.

Her mother was perfectionistic and belittling. There was little Becky could do to please her mom, and it was far safer for Becky to hide in a closet than to disrupt the order of the house. She remembers being rarely physically touched by her mother when she was suffering.

Becky and I were a couple whose past harm fit like a charm. I had been grooved by a thousand events to live on the edge but also trained to be ridiculously attuned to the sound of a voice, the shifting topography of the face, and the implied desires never stated. I was more attentive to Becky than she had ever experienced in any relationship.

Becky had been swimming in the waters of unpredictability and eccentric playfulness all her life and was highly accustomed to rage and violence. So my unusual approach to having fun and my flashes of anger were no more disconcerting than what she had suffered throughout her upbringing.

For me, Becky was fascinated by my stories, just like my mom and dad had been—but she offered the benefit of never needing me to fix, placate, or soothe her. She was utterly intact and independent, yet thrilled with my playful, eccentric attention.

Our past trauma carved us to fit so perfectly it looked like an act of God. The only problem was, we didn't know we had trauma, or that what we each wanted was redemption from the past. All we could see was a bright, exhilarating future.

That was true until what we each unwittingly demanded from the other was derailed by our loyalty to our unaddressed trauma and our families.

Discovering What Rules and Divides Us

Like all young couples, Becky and I were intoxicated by each other.[1] This dating period for all of us is equivalent to being high on cocaine, as we bounce above reality on a combination of oxytocin and dopamine. We are literally high for six to ten months in the early bonding period. Eventually, the body regulates and produces less ebullient biochemicals, and reality dawns.

The reality for Becky and me was that just because we were engaged, and then married, my mother was no less crazy and my father no more willing to engage with her erratic behavior, including her newfound competition with my wife. I still felt my role was to keep my mother sane, soothe her with stories, and bear the Atlantic storms that would sweep through our winter.

Becky's insistence that I was, first and foremost, her husband felt to me like a demand to juggle a buzz saw, a bowling ball, and a new wife—to somehow keep them all in the air at once. I was enraged at what I perceived to be Becky's weakness and need (I'd been counting on her being independent, the opposite of my mother). How could I possibly keep both my mother and my wife satisfied? The more I felt out of control, the more rage I expressed to Becky.

Her response to my anger was to shut down, freeze, and glare. She would walk away from a fight, then I would intensify. My intensification would hit a stone wall, and I'd feel terrified and desperate.

In those moments, we lived a thousand miles from each other's hearts.

After spending hours or days on separate continents (emotionally speaking), we would find our way back to each other and slowly return to touch. The debris from our collision was swept away, never truly addressed, and a demilitarized zone (DMZ) was formed—meaning, we learned to avoid talking about her family or mine.

Becky's role in her family was to comfort her father and avoid her mother. If I approached an aspect of her loyalty to her father that seemed in competition with me, our intimacy went to hell. If she touched on my mother's craziness and my frantic, angry efforts to soothe her, we entered an even deeper ring of hell. Hell competed with our efforts to create heaven.

Every couple struggles to some degree with leaving the psychological and relational demands of their family of origin. As much as I loved Becky, I was more loyal to the role and demands of my family, especially my mother. As much as Becky loved me, she was more loyal to being the bright sunlight for her father. We didn't know it, but we were in a war of trauma built on the foundation of false loyalty to our parents, and leaving it felt like a form of death.

Becky and I can articulate all of this to you now, but at the time, we were *clueless* about what was going on. We were breaking each other's hearts without having the insight to understand why or the language to deal with it.

We did not see that we had married each other to escape our trauma, or that marrying each other did not, necessarily, enable us to break free from our families and past trauma.

We married each other to redeem what we had lost and suffered *without naming* what had driven us into the arms of the other—which meant our deep hurts kept hurting. And ruling us. And dividing us.

We married each other to find God and, in turn, at times, we tasted hell.

Our story may be more extreme than yours, but after counseling more than a thousand couples, I know this to be true: what draws couples together eventually can divide them. What brings them together is a hunger for redemption of harm they barely can see, let alone name—and that *failure to name* creates a framework for untold present and future suffering to play out.

To go forward, we must first go back. We must enter the fray of past heartache to have the capacity to dream and live out a radical new future.

Look at How You Two Fit

As I said in the previous chapter, Becky and I have progressed and transformed to an almost unbelievable extent over five decades. As I now stare at my stunning seventy-one-year-old wife in her white corduroys and wool sweater making breakfast as I write this chapter, not only am I not the same man and not in the same marriage I once was, but far more, I have a taste of heaven. And it is only because at some point along the way we started building awareness by looking back, understanding our hurts and tendencies, and seeing what needed tending to.

So I invite you now to start looking back at your own story. Begin with the family dynamic in your upbringing. What were you accustomed to? What was your role? Identify the behaviors you did repeatedly in response to people around you and how you coped with fears or unmet needs. See if you can spot ways you continually felt hurt or frustrated and what longings developed as a result.

Next, think back to when you met your spouse. Maybe it was at school or church, at a bar or a wedding, through online dating or an awkward blind date. No matter where you met, there was a magnetic energy that both propelled you toward each other and created tensions between you. There are those who know after a single minute, *This is the one.* Others knew in the first few minutes, *I'd rather be skinned alive than be with you*, but somehow, against all odds, reason, or sensibility, they married.

The question *How did you meet?* must be asked in light of what drew you to each other. You met scores of people you might have married, but you didn't. The answers I have heard when I've asked this question often boil down to something physical, relational, and spiritual.

"We just clicked."

Or, "We were at loggerheads from the beginning, but something still felt right."

Or, "I don't know other than it just felt inevitable."

What is truly inevitable is, "What I need fits what I think you can provide, and thus I will demand it from you"—and, again, this is all subconscious. The fit is far deeper than what most of us have considered.

I want you to celebrate the odd, lovely, and, at times, crazy ways God brought you into the sphere of your spouse. It wasn't an accident. But it is far more than merely God's will. Our movement toward each other includes our felt need for restoring, our longing for the other to replenish what we sense we lack.

No matter how close to or divided from your spouse you feel today, can you remember the days and hours of your beginning? What new life did they bring to your existence that felt intoxicating? Usually the process is jagged and does not follow a logical, linear route, but can you trace the steps that brought you to the greatest risk of your life, when you said yes?

Even more, can you peek behind the curtain on stage and ask, What did I see or feel or hope that my spouse might restore and replenish that I lacked, or only fleetingly enjoyed, in my family of origin?

The hardest work ahead is to explore how the heartache, hurt, and trauma you both endured created the context for how you used to fit together. If at any point this exploration feels daunting, remind yourself of this: the journey ahead is the path to true restoration, replenishment, and intimacy.

three

Digging Under the Surface

Steve

*When you open your heart to discovery, you will
be called to step outside the comfort barriers
within which you have fortified your life.*

JOHN O'DONOHUE

When I first saw Lisa at age sixteen, I was stunned and in awe. I remember the moment as if it were yesterday, even though it was more than forty years ago. Her face radiated joy, and I was utterly captivated. Within minutes, I tepidly moved toward her to ask if she would sign my yearbook.

We began dating in our junior year of high school and became inseparable. We lost track of time when we were together; nothing else mattered in the dopamine high of early intimacy. Even so, we became an on-again, off-again couple. I genuinely loved her, but I was cautious, immature, and couldn't make up my mind.

Our breakups left us feeling lonely, so we'd get back together, but before long, I'd hear myself say, "Maybe we should date other people."

Lisa's response would be akin to the iconic words of Taylor Swift: "We are never, ever getting back together."

But of course, we did.

My love for Lisa only grew stronger with time; her beauty, kindness, and tenderness increasingly grabbed my heart. I knew there was no one I'd rather spend my life with when I married her at age twenty-two.

Lisa was what my own mother was not, which I found deeply attractive. My mother was frequently distracted and emotionally unavailable; at other times, she was emotionally demanding, requiring me to be supportive in ways my father was not. At an early age, I learned there was little room for me to express my needs, so I became fiercely independent.

Though I didn't realize it in the early stages of dating and married life, I was attracted to Lisa's lack of emotional need for me. (Yes, coincidentally, Dan and I both felt drawn to women who did not exude "neediness.") Lisa's story was similar to mine in that she experienced emotional neglect in her family of origin and learned to be self-sufficient. The primary message we both internalized was *do not need*.

So I went into marriage feeling like I'd hit the jackpot—here was a gorgeous woman I loved who didn't demand attention or reassurance. I had the illusion that marriage offered a "need-free" zone, a liberating arrangement that offered emotional connection without demands. Little did I know that Lisa's and my pattern of denying our needs would lead us away from true joy and deep intimacy.

On top of that, we'd been heavily influenced by the purity culture movement and were convinced that all would be bliss in the early days of marriage. Between that and our unacknowledged expectation that we'd each somehow intuitively provide for the other what was missing in our upbringings, Lisa and I were in for some surprises.

In the last chapter we asked you to look at how you functioned in your family of origin and what drew you to your spouse, including the ways you perhaps unconsciously hoped to find healing. Now, we will look at how the story progressed from there, at the relational dynamic within a marriage (especially after the oxytocin and dopamine of early togetherness wore off).

Dan and I help couples become aware of what's contributing to the disconnection and distress they are experiencing. Most couples struggle in one or more of the following ways (which certainly has been true for Lisa and me): *a lack of delight, loneliness, contempt,* and *feeling stuck.* We're going to look closely at each one of these in this chapter.

If you do not find yourself in these experiences, know there is value in continuing the journey with us. I believe all of us, at some point, will be able to relate to something here. Coming to understand these issues now will help you navigate them whenever you encounter them and move into deeper intimacy.

Lack of Delight

Marco and Marie would each tell you they married their best friend. No one could make Marco laugh like Marie. No one could make Marie feel as free as Marco. The early years were filled with adventures, game nights, and dinner dates. Further down the road now, they get along fine, but something is missing. Marco wonders what has changed, where all the fun, excitement, and playfulness went. Is it the weight of more responsibilities, the constant distractions of life, or the inevitable effects of getting older? Surely the beginning doesn't have to be the best part of their story, does it?

He wants their relationship to spark delight in his heart and brighten her face.

Delight is far more than mere happiness, optimism, or positivity. It comes from gratitude founded in a sense of wonder. It is a childlike joy in the beauty of a moment that surprises us with goodness we can only receive and not demand.

I sense delight when my four-year-old grandson runs to me and says, "Push me on the swing, Papa." Then, as his body flies through the air and I gently tickle him when he floats by, his face shines, and his ringing giggles surround us.

Amid our busy life, Lisa sometimes will pause and pull me in for a warm embrace, gently reminding me with both touch and words, "I like being with you." Then I'll be flooded with delight in her generous gift of tenderness and closeness.

More than any other emotion, delight can come quickly and unexpectedly, then depart just as rapidly. It is a fleeting taste of eternity, elusive, compelling, and life-giving.

And it is meant to be part of our marriages.

No one experiences near-constant joy in their marriage, but sadly, some of us go long stretches with little to no delight. While even in a strong relationship, it may be relatively infrequent, joy is never meant to be rare. We have learned to deny the desire to be delighted in, but it exists in every heart.

Loneliness

Victoria and her husband have had conversations every day this week, but they have yet to truly connect. They've brushed their teeth beside each other, shared meals at the table, and ended their days in the same bed. Yet what Victoria longs for most is for him to put down his phone or step away from his tasks and offer her his full attention. To stop everything else and look her in the eyes—not so they can discuss a mundane house repair or decide on dinner time, but so they can really see each other.

She's not sure when she last felt truly known by him.

Our core desire is to be seen and desired. *Do you really want to be with me? Do I need to do something for you or entertain you for you to want to be with me?* Few of us believe that we are enough to warrant being chosen; we are convinced we must "earn" care.

We are accustomed to social situations where no one is intrigued enough to ask us thoughtful questions and listen to our responses. Instead, we engage in surface conversations that overall are fine but leave us with a twinge of loneliness.

We are created to know and be known. You are known when someone becomes attuned to the inner workings of your heart (your emotions, thoughts, desires, struggles) and learns to read your face, body, words, and tone.

This requires intention, attention, and desire. It calls the human heart to give another its presence. As difficult as it is to define what this means, we know when someone is fully open, committed, and captured by us versus engaging for their own benefit or for the sake of accomplishing a task. It goes beyond the normal fare of chatting about the calendar, offering opinions, or asking for the salt to be passed. Presence communicates, "I choose you."

Over a morning cup of coffee with Lisa, I was distracted by my phone for a while. Lisa was quiet, then offered gently, "Steve, when you are on your phone while we're having coffee, I feel a bit lonely." Presence is giving the other our face. It is our face, our presence, that keeps our heart from feeling lonely.

Contempt

Carlos watches his wife pour her attention and love on their children—games, toys, and outings. It's beautiful. It's Instagram worthy. And it has completely changed their relationship. She once shined all that enthusiasm and delight in his direction; now he's getting a steady stream of exasperation. To her, he's the parent who never does things "right" and keeps pushing her buttons.

He longs for her irritation to fall away, for her to see all his effort, and for her to let him in.

One of our greatest fears is to be shamed and humiliated, and tragically, many of us experience this in marriage.

We may sense a low register of irritation and disapproval in our daily exchanges or a more explicit version. "I feel like I'm never doing things right," Carlos told me. "My wife is my judge and jury. I know I'll be blamed and found guilty when anything goes wrong."

He would huff and puff, throw up his hands in exasperation, and, barely under his breath, berate her for being thoughtless or stupid. When she would address his frustration, he would dismiss her as oversensitive, claiming she was overreacting to his legitimate concerns. She learned it was easier to swallow his complaining and ignore his demeaning judgments.

Contempt sets out to control another's behavior through shaming and belittling. It can be as subtle as raising an eyebrow or as overt as screaming obscenities; either way, it intends to make the other feel foolish and unlovable.

Contempt often causes partners to form DMZs—areas of conflict that they avoid at all costs. (You might recall the description of the DMZ Becky and Dan formed around the issues of their parents in the last chapter.) Contempt warns the other that silence and compliance are better than all-out war. *Surrender your desire for change rather than enter the dangerous terrain and encounter another blow-up.*

Most marriages have one person who leans toward other-centered contempt and one who is prone to self-contempt. One person blames; the other accepts the fault (at least outwardly). If the DMZ is avoided and the partner with self-contempt keeps assuming the lion's share of the blame, the couple can get along fine. Eventually, however, they will stumble into the DMZ, and when the blamer reacts explosively and hurls more judgment at the other, all matters of hell break loose.

Feeling Stuck

Shandra tells her friends that she and her husband have ups and downs, like any couple. What she doesn't say is that they've been "down" for years.

That they've had the same argument a hundred times. That their dynamic is an unending merry-go-round of struggle, and her once-visceral frustration has been replaced with hopeless resignation. It'll never change. This is who they are. It's okay, Shandra tells herself. Her kids, her job, her friends . . . they can be her life. They can be enough.

She desires so much more for them but can't bear to let herself admit it.

We all know what it's like to feel stuck in some area of life. The harder we try and the less success we experience, the more we want to give up—and the more we learn to hate or diminish our desire. *If I don't want, I don't hurt. If I accept this as inevitable, I can endure my situation and pursue whatever pleasure is within reach.*

There are two results for marriages in which one or both partners have attempted to change and have experienced little or no growth: distractions and addiction. We avoid their heartache and create a parallel life where we can find moments of relief. This outside focus—whether it is a job, a hobby, a degree program, an affair, pornography, or one's children—can become a consuming idol.

We protect ourselves from ongoing frustration and hurt when we know nothing will change while also subtly or strategically saying to our spouses: *I no longer choose you.* It feels like an almost necessary choice to direct our focus elsewhere, but it is not. It is a way to create distance from our pain and experience temporary relief.

The Roots Below: Unaddressed Trauma

We hurt in these areas in obvious ways, but *we also hurt in deeper places in hidden ways.* Lack of delight, loneliness, contempt, and feeling stuck are the symptoms that are wearing us down, and *they're connected to something at the core of us*: unaddressed trauma.

We've discussed how we brought unconscious longings into marriages and that our brokenness unwittingly played a part in our attraction to our partners. These realities were part of our relational dynamic in the beginning, and they remain with us throughout the years. Again, what draws us together can eventually divide us—unless we become aware of the deeper issues at play.

Surface stressors or distractions, such as our jobs, children, finances, or health problems, contribute to relational tension, but they are not the root cause. The bigger issue is that we are unconsciously feeling the disappointment of, *I believed you'd always give me what I needed, and now you are failing me. I also sense that I'm failing you too.* This disappointment is deeply, almost perplexingly, intertwined with our unaddressed trauma.

These four issues—lack of delight, loneliness, contempt, and feeling stuck—are the weeds we see on the surface. But if we dig down and address the unseen root cause, it will no longer prevent good fruit from flourishing in our relationship.

Let's briefly revisit those four issues and consider how past trauma is often linked to them. And again, even if you do not identify with any of these issues today, I invite you to linger in this conversation. We will soon move into broad concepts that will equip every couple—whatever their situation—who is longing to develop deeper intimacy and generate new goodness between them and beyond them.

Lack of Delight

Unresolved trauma steals delight and makes it feel unreachable. Trauma-bound hearts seldom move toward thriving as insecurity and a sense of "goodness sparsity" pervades. We focus on controlling what we can and preserving what we have through self-protective behaviors. We settle for simply surviving when vastly more is available to us in marriage.

Delight can't be summoned, but we are meant to prepare for its arrival, like placing an extra setting on the dinner table for a special guest. We can do so by regularly being caught up in gratitude, the foundation of delight. Even if the gifts in life are small and incidental, the heart is meant to receive them with gratitude.

The more grateful we are for our spouses, the more fertile the ground becomes for growing delight. Even when I feel angry with Lisa or hurt by her, I also can feel thankful that the desire for delight has not died and that what is exposed in us both may lead us to greater intimacy.

Many of us experienced a subtle dismissal of delight in our upbringing, as we felt more like an inconvenience than a joy to our parents. Marriage can bring into our present what was missing in our past, as we sense from our spouses, *I delight in you.*

Only when we have a greater goal than control or comfort can we experience gratitude and delight. It's when we are following the invitation to taste God's goodness and embrace who we are meant to be in our fullness as loved and loving human beings.

Loneliness

When you were a child, how often did the face of your primary caregivers seem distracted, ambivalent, irritated, or distant? Was it rare for someone to offer you presence?

The lack of emotional presence is the trauma of abandonment, which can seem too severe to name unless a parent leaves a child for days without care. But the reality is, most parents are too busy to offer their presence, and the absence of attentive care and consistent, intentional reading of your face and heart has a lingering traumatic impact.

It may not seem dramatic or unusual, but it affects us all the same. It is like the ground where chemicals have been dumped and have seeped into drinking water. Seldom will there be immediate consequences, but the failure, if never addressed, will result in toxic water that eventually causes disease.

Loneliness is no different. When we feel lonely, distant, or continually distracted, it is not merely an issue of being busy or overwhelmed; it is an indication of unaddressed trauma.[1]

Contempt

A couple who has built their equilibrium on the use of contempt will build layer upon layer of hurt and disappointment. When it surfaces, it will feel like nothing will restore the relationship—not apologies, remorse, or good intentions. The issue is seldom only what is occurring in the marriage. These patterns involve histories related to shame and humiliation in our families of origin, perhaps abuse and rejection during heightened periods of vulnerability. We hide ourselves in contempt to escape the residual effects of shame from countless earlier experiences.

People often try to address the patterns of shame and contempt in their marriage by only looking at the present, but they need to go deeper, to the roots of past trauma, in order to experience change.

Feeling Stuck

We all adopted roles in our family of origin; we settled into behaviors that allowed us to function and survive in that setting. If we made attempts to change our roles, we may have felt a hostile force against it from our families and that we had no option but to acquiesce, even if it hurt. We learned to do what was expected while hiding our desires.

Our compliance led to exhaustion and self-judgment. We coped by finding some relief in an outside source, something else we felt offered us life.

The greater the loss and suffering we experienced, the more we trusted something else to comfort us and help us escape. We ate ourselves back to peace. We masturbated ourselves back to love. We focused intensely on our music, video games, or books. We found things to take us away from our pain and give us a moment of pleasure.

It is likely that we brought these same coping mechanisms into adulthood and into our marriages.

When we first experienced intimacy with our spouses, our exciting connection made all things new. Whatever we used for coping in the past held little interest—but only until an unaddressed past trauma surfaced.

Amid disappointment and conflict, a deep issue we couldn't face was exposed and intensified. To cope, we returned to whatever helped us in the past. While we're doing what feels intrinsic to us, we're carrying out patterns of distraction or addiction, which are signs of unaddressed hurt.

Dealing with the Present Means Addressing the Past

At this point in the chapter, some of your experiences may be coming to mind. You may be starting the courageous, worthy task of honest reflection. If so, I applaud you.

I also will mention that most of us are biased toward feeling that our partners are the primary source of any problems in our marriages. Dan and I have been there. I've become preoccupied with Lisa's failures as a way to cope with my past. And I regularly see couples come to therapy with the conviction that if their partner would do x and not y, then their own missteps (which they somewhat acknowledge but quickly justify) would melt in the noonday summer sun, and all would be well.

It is natural to feel this way, but it's simply not true. No one in a marriage is faultless. No one is meant to "win" or be deemed always right. Both partners are human and on a path of growth. Both are, in some way, failing the other—and this is not a shameful discovery but a common reality with imperfect people, one we can learn to address graciously and grow from.

You and your partner's failure of each other is incredibly complex, tangled up with your deeply held ways of being in the world and the relational patterns you each developed in response to trauma throughout your lives. You learned to survive through an unconscious process of mitigating hurt and finding solace through some internal means. You still function within those patterns today as you navigate life, instinctively reacting to friction and trying to regulate yourselves.

It is likely that, in the tension of conflict with your spouse, you feel it isn't possible to address your past trauma. Perhaps it rarely comes up, and when it does, it is used as a basis for blame, not empathy. Whatever the case, know this: *if you are willing to address the past, you will be far more equipped to deal with the present.*

We are not responsible for what happened to us, but we are meant to own and engage our past and its impact, especially in the ways it influences our sense of self and our style of relating today. In the coming chapters, we will unpack all this, looking at it from various angles and unveiling its many layers.

Change Agents

Along the way, Dan and I will steer you toward *change agents*, the key attitudes that lead us into transformation.

Before I list them, I want to acknowledge that, for some of you, they may read like a fantasy, like a distant mirage with no bearing on your reality. Reading them may even, at first, feel disorienting. But remember the longing for intimacy and healing. For *more.* Be assured that you can move at your own pace. Then give yourself permission to imagine experiencing them. *What if they are livable?*

The truth is, we all can experience them, even if it means weeks or months of inching in their direction first. Wherever you and your partner are today, Dan and I desire to help you move toward each other, one chapter at a time. For now, we're inviting you to open your mind and heart to them. To wonder and imagine the possibilities. Here are the change agents we'll discuss.

> **Humility**: the ability to be attuned and aware of what is happening in myself and the other; to disrupt the triggering of trauma, past and present

Honesty: the resolve to own what is mine and to engage without blaming the other for what I feel; to address the "log in my own eye" first (Matthew 7:3–5)

Kindness: a fierce commitment to enter the heartache and fear of the other with compassion and care

Curiosity: the intentional entering into the story and experience of the other, which will develop a desire to know and understand what the other feels, desires, and fears

Defiance: a refusal to let hurt, anger, and past failure to determine the future of what we are able to create together; a stance of "hell, no" to death in all its forms (whatever hardens us and keeps us from having a life of connection between us)

Intention to bless: holding the other in and with wonder and awe, delight and gratitude; a stance of "heaven, yes" to the beauty we can create together

These are not attitudes for us to conjure on our own, nor are they simply behaviors for us to learn to perform. These are depictions of the Spirit of the living God at work in us, of a God whose nature is unlike our own. When we create space for him to come close, to love us and lead us, we can lean into what he reveals.

We are pursuing true heart change in both partners.

We are on a journey of discovering God's purposes for love, finding opportunities for redemptive moments, and ultimately choosing to write a new marriage story. It may feel implausible—but, believe me, it is not too hard for the one known for bringing life to the valley of dry bones. The one who gives you breath moment after moment also can cause you to flourish.

Let's close this chapter with a truth to sit with and try to absorb, as we step forward, a reality that perhaps you feel hesitant to receive or seems too good to be true.

God's heart is full of tenderness toward you.

He's gazing at you with love and compassion. He sees your hurts. He validates them, even feels them with you.

Envision his tenderness softening you, and you opening your heart and looking at it with him. Imagine him showing you what needs to heal and strengthening your will to thrive in new ways. And perhaps even ask for his heart attitude to become more a part of you and for him to stay close as you turn the pages.

A Note from Lisa

I n the first years of my relationship with Steve, I felt more known than I ever had before. He delighted in me and was attuned to me beyond what I ever had imagined for myself. I was head over heels in love.

While I couldn't see it at the time, the four categories discussed in this chapter were at play in our dynamic from the beginning, as we dated and broke up more than a handful of times. Our bodies were trying to interpret mixed signals: *I am safe* and *I am not safe.* But our lack of delight, our loneliness, our stuckness, and our contempt (for ourselves and for one another) stemmed from the traumas we experienced individually before we met.

When I first learned about naming trauma from my family of origin, I felt unsure and hesitant about it. *I grew up in a strong, loving, Christian family. What else is there to say?*

But over the years, there was a loneliness that haunted me. I could not make sense of its nagging heaviness in my life. I seemingly had it all—a good husband, children, friends, job, ministry, and church—and yet it plagued me.

When our third child was born, I could no longer ignore it, and I developed postpartum depression. It was a very lonely time for me as well as for Steve. He felt that he could not get access to me.

All four of these categories were part of our struggle.

I felt unlovable and, therefore, lacked and could not communicate delight.

I struggled daily with feeling alone.

Steve and I became stuck in a cycle of blame, which led to contempt.

I resented him for not having more capacity to parent or for spending time with friends.

I felt contempt toward myself for being unable to be what Steve needed. Even the fact that I had *need* made me feel like a failure. I was desperate to be self-sufficient because "not having needs" helped me cope in childhood (meanwhile, acknowledging my need was the very thing I needed to do to survive in our marriage). I could not see or express any of this at the time; I just felt miserable in an unbearable cycle.

Around this time, Steve and Dan were teaching a marriage workshop, and Steve and I began paying closer attention to our families of origin. We started sharing simple stories from our childhoods we hadn't shared before and discussing ways we experienced conflict and intimacy.

I told Steve how, as a child in my family, we did not dialogue about conflict; we merely waited in silence for it to pass. Consequently, silence feels confusing and lonely for me as an adult.

Steve shared with me that in his family, when conflict erupted, his mom often looked to him for comfort, even when he was a young boy. Consequently, when he senses I need comfort or reassurance, it can feel like a demand.

During this time, I began to see the juxtaposition of my longing for emotional connection and my family's lack of emotional availability. Even though my parents were generally there for me physically, they rarely offered me emotional presence, and I developed a sense of deep loneliness.

It was as if I had been "trained" in my family of origin that emotional needs were unacceptable. I learned that it was more desirable to have family peace than to make my emotional needs known. So I ignored my feelings—especially hurt, sadness, and anger—and pushed them down deep. I always tried to be "the good girl" who avoided further conflict and used distraction and humor to keep the peace.

By the time Steve and I met at age sixteen, I had developed a significant distance from my emotional needs—which worked out perfectly for Steve. He was attracted to this part of me that appeared to have no needs. He had developed a similar style of coping, so our compatibility seemed off the charts as we rode off into the sunset. But of course, our fierce commitment to being "independent" and "self-sufficient" quickly unraveled.

Amid the inevitable stressors of life, our self-protecting behaviors (tied to our past traumas) surfaced. When we began to express our needs and feelings, we felt exposed, inadequate, and confused. Our frustrations came out in accusatory demands and blaming, and, as I described above, we experienced all four of these categories in significant ways throughout many years of marriage.

Our turning point came when we started understanding ourselves and one another in the context of our stories. That is what set us on an entirely different trajectory, prompting incredible healing in us individually and profound restoration in our relationship. Today we are able to be curious and kind to each other in ways we had never known was possible, and there is more vibrancy and new strength in our connection.

Maybe you are like me and feel hesitant to name and address trauma. You might have had wonderful parents, and nothing major stands out to you. I encourage you to remain curious, even if it is uncomfortable or seems pointless. Your parents may have done their best, but you likely still will find areas in your young life where you felt unseen, fearful, or hurt without comfort. Heavy burdens are sometimes inadvertently placed on young children for the family's survival. Sometimes generations of harm and trauma have unexpected trickle-down effects.

Naming your trauma can feel harsh, judgmental, and dishonorable to those who raised you. But the goal here is not to cast blame; it is to explore the impact of your experiences and how they have shaped you.

Choosing this path has helped me pay attention to my feelings and learn to communicate them to Steve. His kindness and curiosity have invited me to be present with my difficult emotions and acknowledge wounds that need healing. As we address the past, we find ourselves more equipped in our present relationship; we have more space for humility, honesty, kindness, curiosity, defiance, and intention to bless one another.

It is genuinely a redemptive journey. And how else could we experience it without first knowing what needed to be redeemed?

four

Seeing Your Own Trauma

*Man, the bravest animal and most prone to suffer, does
not deny suffering as such: he wills it, he even seeks it out,
provided he is shown a meaning for it, a purpose of suffering.*

FRIEDRICH NIETZSCHE

You and I are meant for honor and delight.[1]

We are meant to be treated with genuine care and respect. To encounter people and places that stir profound awe and joy in us. To experience Eden.

Today, we are not in the original Eden of the past or the restored Eden of the future. We can get glimpses of that abundant beauty, but we live in what theologians call the "already and not yet." While the kingdom of God is here now, its consummation—the full restoration of the earth and all who live in it—has yet to occur. And in this era of the in-between, we all know suffering. We all experience trauma.

But let us swiftly move from that bleak reality to this bright one: *Our trauma does not have to be the undoing of us.*

We can walk the path of healing, know deep connectedness, even experience transformation—if only we will address our trauma with brave honesty and consistent care. There is pain, yes; but there is also hope for beauty, meaning, and joy. We have the option of inviting the kingdom of God into our deepest places.

Perhaps you feel the word *trauma* doesn't apply to your story, that it relates only to damages more severe than yours. The truth is, however, that you have known harm, whatever the severity. And what is trauma, exactly?

Trauma is any violation of human dignity that comes through emotional, physical, sexual, or spiritual harm.

It desecrates what was meant to be, leaving a person fragmented, numb, and isolated. Every form of abuse leaves a residue that mars our sense of self and way of relating to others.

We typically ignore our past harm and try to escape it—at times, even unknowingly—which ultimately worsens and multiplies it. This is a theme you will hear often in this book: *Denial or avoidance of what is true inevitably brings about more harm.* As a client once put it, "I'm learning that I either pay now, or I pay even more later."

We can choose either to sit in the discomfort of honesty and humbly acknowledge our pain now, or go on deepening and spreading our heartache.

Wounds That Keep Hurting

Let me introduce you to one couple who spent the first decade of their marriage avoiding their past wounds.

Janet is a quiet, watchful, avoidant woman who works hard to resolve conflict and tension before it can get out of hand. Her friends consider her to be a good listener and highly sensitive, and never demanding or intrusive. They find it hard to get to know her, however, because she seldom shares an opinion or desire. Janet married Jon, a man who couldn't be more different.

Jon is articulate, opinionated, and, if questioned or criticized, becomes defensive and cruel. Whereas Janet is more introverted and selects only a few friends, he is gregarious and outgoing, and drives their social life with his many friends and acquaintances.

Jon initially loved Janet's quiet strength and supportive presence, but over time he tired of trying to initiate conversation. Janet loved Jon's rich relational world and the intrigue he created with his adventurous risk-taking, but she was soon exhausted by his drama, intensity, and periodic explosions.

Jon was bored and chronically irritated with Janet, and she was confused, lonely, and overwhelmed by all the conflict that resulted from her failed attempts to improve their relationship. What had never been addressed was the weighty heartache they'd *brought into the marriage*.

Janet came from an alcoholic family that covered up their addiction with a rigorous facade of upper-middle-class success. She was the youngest child and had two older brothers. The oldest began to sexually abuse her when she was eight and he was fourteen. Her father was her ally, but was seldom home. Her mother, often intoxicated and depressed, found fault with her in nearly every area of her life. Young Janet was expected to help cover for her mother's failures by taking the blame for everything.

Young Jon, on the other hand, was the prince for his mother and two years younger than his brother. Jon was asthmatic, physically small through most of his first sixteen years, and considered by his peers to be effeminate and bookish. His older brother was a superb athlete, hated school, and got in trouble with teachers, but he kept progressing under the tutelage of his coaches. His father was his biggest supporter and spent vastly more time with him than with Jon, so Jon spent countless hours reading and talking with his mom.

Young Jon suffered repetitive bullying from his brother and his friends. He was often the butt of foul humor in his classroom but was protected by teachers who found him delightful and bright.

Both Jon and Janet knew a cursory history of each other's past, but they had never reflected on how their past trauma was playing out in their current conflicts.

Let's go back to what trauma is and how it affects us.

Trauma is any violation of human dignity that comes through emotional, physical, sexual, or spiritual harm. It desecrates what was meant to be, leaving the person fragmented, numb, and isolated. Every form of abuse leaves a residue that mars our sense of self and way of relating to others.

Some of our harm appears subtle and insignificant (small-t trauma) whereas other events are overtly and obviously violating (what we'll call capital-T Trauma). We generally fail to see small-t trauma and diminish the importance of what we intuitively know left scars.

Abuse is seldom singular or isolated from other forms of harm. A person who is sexually abused is also likely emotionally, physically, and spiritually harmed as well. Bullying is both emotional and physical and often degrades the victim's sexual identity. Physical abuse seldom occurs without emotional abuse, just as spiritual abuse always involves some degree of emotional violation.

Abuse is always traumatizing whether we own the wounds or not.

What exactly does abuse look like? To answer that, we will need to understand various forms of it so we can better identify it in our stories.

Emotional Abuse

Words cut to the quick when their intention is either to cut down our confidence or humiliate us. Small-t trauma from emotional abuse occurs when our dignity is undermined by snarky criticism or barely hidden contempt.

I once walked into a coffee shop and ran into a friend I had not seen in years. I was thrown when he told me, "Well, you're looking a little worn in the tooth and showing your age." He likely considered it to be playful teasing, and, while it was true, it was a belittling thing to say. Small emotional violations like this are very common. We are, in fact, so accustomed to them that we seldom register anything other than a passing twinge.

I will return to what I said earlier: *We are meant for honor and delight.* We are impacted by mistreatment for valid reason.

When I saw my friend, I felt a warmth of recognition and the anticipation of catching up. But after his slight, I found it difficult to take pleasure in his company and instinctively became guarded and detached. Small-t trauma from emotional harm warns a person to watch their step and not get too close.

Jon would occasionally say to his wife, Janet, "Are you eating a lot of chips?" with a tone of accusation. In Jon's case, his question had little to do with regard for her health and was a means of more covert diminishment. These words are somewhere between small-t trauma and capital-T Trauma.

He also once said to her, "You look so ugly in that outfit. I can't believe how you've let yourself go." Here we have moved clearly into capital-T emotional Trauma. The comment was cruel and insulting, and the effect was humiliation. When the result is someone feeling shame, capital-T Trauma is occurring.

For Jon, this was a passing observation that he claimed had no purpose other than to help Janet lose some weight. For Janet, it echoed many of the cutting remarks she heard from her mother and brother as a child. Her mother was bonded to her brother who sexually abused young Janet, and when her brother was verbally abusive, her mother often blamed Janet rather than protect her.

Jon's harsh remark triggered Janet, and she shut down for days. Yet she never made the connection between Jon's diminishing words and her family of origin's diminishing words. While others looking in might be able to spot patterns, we tend not to see how our past is refracting in our present.

If we have known shame as a long-term effect from countless inter-actions, it is possible for small-t trauma to provoke monumental shame. Tragically the shame-prone person is often told, "You are overreacting—this is not that big of a deal." Capital-T Trauma from shame grooves us to respond to lesser offenses as intense violations.

Part of why Janet shut down was because, deep down, she instinctively believed she deserved the harsh treatment. Emotional abuse often causes the one subjected to humiliation to assume it is their fault. Even when the perpetrator is cruel and violent, the natural response of the abused is to accept the blame and develop self-contempt. Self-contempt joins the abuser through an inner dialogue of faultfinding that explains and perhaps even justifies the demeaning treatment. In turn, self-contempt deepens the wound and begins to rot away at one's sense of goodness and beauty, leaving a person feeling too shameful to name the violation. It is tragic that, often, an emotionally abused person will choose a spouse that is quicker to criticize and demean than to honor and delight—because it is such a familiar dynamic.

It is one of the most important tasks for both partners to reckon with how the experience of emotional abuse and humiliation has been unwit-tingly woven into their marriage.

Physical Abuse

Young Jon was once surrounded by a few larger boys who taunted him on a neighborhood sidewalk. As they ridiculed him for being a wimp, he felt woefully intimidated and darted toward a random house to knock on its front door, even though he didn't know anyone who lived there. Small-t trauma from physical abuse involves intimidation and a subtle threat that physical harm is about to occur.

Young Jon lived with the daily threat of physical or psychological abuse from his brother and his brother's friends. His solace was his good standing with teachers and the emotional support he received from his lonely mother. The family was divided. His father was enamored by his athletic older brother. His mom was more deeply bonded with Jon than she was with her husband or Jon's brother.

Jon was not unaware of the favoritism his mom showed him, yet he never connected that closeness to his brother's rage and envy. He never faced his father's resentment toward him due to his role as his mother's confidant and chief cheerleader, which exceeded the intimacy shared between his mother and father.

We don't like looking at the destructive tendencies of our families, nor can we typically see how those stories play out with our spouses.

It took adult Jon a long time to grasp that the goal of intimidation is to gain mastery over another and force compliance. It took even longer for him to see how he was using words to intimidate and humiliate his wife, just as his brother had done with him years before.

Capital-T Trauma–causing physical abuse is intended to exert mastery while also overtly degrading the victim (though it is easy for those who've been harmed to dismiss it as unintentional). To slap a child in the face is not merely to deliver pain, but to attack their sense of identity. To have a child cut the switch used to blight their flesh is to make them complicit in their harm. To deprive a person of food while others eat is punishment of degradation and deprivation. These are "normal" discipline techniques found in many homes over centuries that are not only considered effective, but also legitimate and benign.

There are, of course, far more egregious forms of physical abuse that literally leave marks for a lifetime. But *all forms* of physical abuse and bullying leave scars that suggest our bodies are not our own and perhaps even deficient somehow. We come to believe we are fragile, vulnerable, and a mark for more harm. It is not hard to see why the combination of emotional and physical abuse leaves a person susceptible to trying to avoid all conflict—or to taking the opposite path of feeling immune to pain and recklessly entering conflict with bravado. These two ways of being are often called *flight* or *fight*.

Sexual Abuse

There is no violation that engenders more shame than sexual abuse. There are varying degrees of sexual abuse, but it is important to understand that all forms of sexual abuse are an earthquake that shatters and divides the heart. I have worked with victims who were repeatedly raped, and *even they* tended to downplay their harm as they compared it to others who suffered more.

Many people have had an encounter with pornography and have failed to address how it was placed in their hands or before their eyes. Who gave them the explicit sexual material? Who wanted to see them see it? How was the giver aroused by the receiver's intrigue? Giving access to pornography is a form of sexual abuse. It is more subtle but nevertheless devastating—and difficult to address because it seems so "minor" compared to other forms of abuse. We must remember: sexual abuse in any form, subtle or overt, crosses a line of dignity that brings ruin and a loss of innocence.

A significant part of the abuse is what usually occurs before a direct violation: grooming. Grooming is an intentional, seductive act of care and intimacy, like smiling at a student in class when they expect judgment, that elicits trust and increases a desire for more. Grooming is usually so sufficiently hidden and subtle that victims rarely consider what caused them to not say no or report the initial violation.

As egregious as the actual sexual abuse, what lingers for many victims is a hatred of innocence and desire.

Janet once said, "If I wasn't so needy, I wouldn't have been taken in by his warmth." Another client reflected, "I was like a desert that had not seen rain in a decade, so when he watered my soil, flowers burst out that I didn't know that I had." Sexual violation can be confusingly tangled up with attention that meets legitimate emotional needs. And as the violation gets intertwined with emotions that we perceive "allowed" it, we learn to resent them both. We are left with a contemptuous curse against our own vulnerability and desire.

Most victims feel so much shame about their capital-T Trauma that they refuse to name it as sexual abuse. I once worked with a sexual crimes detective who referred to her uncle's sexual abuse as "molestation."

"Why don't you call his touch sexual abuse?" I asked her.

She looked stunned. "But he didn't penetrate me."

"Are the victims you work with considered sexually abused if they aren't penetrated?" I gently pressed.

She again looked incredulous. "Of course they are sexually abused even without penetration."

In the silence that followed, the contradiction finally dawned on her.

"Oh my God, are you saying I have been sexually abused?"

The answer was, of course, yes. The intensity of our shame and dissociation makes our logic fragmented; we fiercely refuse to face reality.

Sexual abuse is a form of possession; it attaches the perpetrator to the victim's pleasure, now and in the future, especially sexual arousal. The abuser is usually insistent that the victim feel some degree of pleasure and offer touch in return that clearly evidences arousal. Whether conscious or not, the perpetrator intends both to possess and ruin the innocence of the victim.

The result in the victim is deep-rooted shame and contempt for one's body, desire, and arousal. It lingers in the extremity of I-am-already-ruined-who-cares sexuality, which is often called immorality, or I-will-not-feel-or-want-arousal prudery, when one self-righteously resolves the shame of the past by maintaining current-day rigidity and anhedonia. In either case, the victim is haunted. Shame is silenced but still screaming.

We have said that young Janet was sexually abused by her brother—it was a clearly recognizable form. Even so, she was profoundly reluctant to enter those stories and face how the harm showed up in her marriage.

Young Jon was sexually abused as well but in a less overt way. He was taunted and physically held down by his brother while his friends pinched Jon's breasts and grabbed his crotch. They all mocked his effeminacy and called him derogatory names. Through these various assaults, they were harming Jon emotionally, physically, and, yes, sexually.

For a long time, adult Jon refused to address the interaction as sexually abusive; he could see it only as a bizarre activity of a crazy, wild older brother and his followers. The implications of this for his present-day sexuality, including the sexual demands he would make of his wife, were essentially off-limits during our therapy sessions.

Spiritual Abuse

Small-t trauma–causing spiritual abuse often comes in the form of familiar presumptions and well-intended practices. When truth is used untruthfully, or said without awareness of a person and their context, it is traumatizing.

For example, a dear friend's husband died unexpectedly, and a well-meaning acquaintance told her, "We just have to trust all things work to the good for those who love God." She was poorly paraphrasing Romans 8:28, and, in the context of the first days of my friend's loss, the truth was spoken without wisdom and sensitivity, making the truth a lie.

Many seem to believe that the height of true love is offering single-verse palliatives to those who are immensely struggling. If we offered aspirin to treat cancer, we would be called foolish. But with spiritual issues, we often fail to diagnose the real "disease," and then we offer solutions that are anything but healing. Physicians who do this are considered guilty of malpractice; yet in spiritual communities, it is fully accepted as good practice.

Small-t trauma–causing spiritual mishaps become more abusive when the "treatment" offered doesn't work. A spiritual leader becomes more insistent and intense with a tone of incrimination. If only you believed more, or did what was suggested, the problem wouldn't remain.

If there is pushback, the small-t trauma perpetrator usually becomes even more domineering and demands acquiescence. The victim ultimately assumes it is easier to give in than to fight. It is easier not to ask questions, so they parrot the dominant theology. We should acknowledge that this is as true of the dogmatism in the fundamentalist, evangelical world as it is the progressive, liberal sphere.

Capital-T Trauma–causing spiritual abuse goes beyond mere pressure to subjugation and severance. When a spiritual leader insists on another's submission to their will—in regard to their beliefs or practices or both—a violation of dignity has occurred.

It is even more egregious when submission to their will is voiced with the authority of God. "God told me that you are not to take that job and move out of your current ministry. If you do so, you will lose all that God has given you." The perpetrator has assumed the knowledge and voice of God with a direct threat against the person if they choose a different direction. This is subjugation.

The difference between small-t spiritual abuse and capital-T spiritual abuse may at first seem too subtle to make a distinction. Small-t abuse often comes in the form of well-meaning counsel or advice. When it is not accepted or followed, the abuser is likely to blame and place greater pressure to do what is demanded. In capital-T abuse the ante is upped to threats, demands, and the prospect of being cast out of fellowship for being recalcitrant. Often the capital-T abuser demands loyalty and crosses boundaries, which they insist must remain secret. It is not uncommon for spiritual abuse to cross over into some form of sexual violation.

It is tragic enough when our spirituality is maligned and undermined, but many have suffered emotional and sexual abuse perpetrated by spiritual leaders. I have worked with many women who were abused by older women who "mentored" them. Because it involved two adult women, it was often considered an affair. When spiritual leaders use their power to groom, arouse, and seduce those under their care, it is sexual abuse—no matter the age or gender of the victim. This is true when the leader is grooming a child in a youth group, and it can also be true when a spiritual leader is sexually involved with an adult in their organization. Even if outsiders simply consider it an affair, it actually can be sexually and spiritually abusive.

Look Closer at Your Story

It is a crucial task to look squarely at abuse, understand it, identify it, and track its impact—but it is weighty. Sometimes excruciating. As we process these hard realities, let's come back to a few bigger, unchanging truths that we can count on no matter what we have been through.

You and I were made in the image of God; we have his imprint on us.

He infused us with immense value and dignity.

He chooses to dwell in us.

He invites us into the joyful, loving community of the Trinity.

He intends us to experience honor and delight.

He names us his beloved.

Even as we may feel far from these beautiful realities, he wants to draw us into them. He relentlessly reaches out to his beloved; he doesn't leave us to be permanently damaged.

With that knowledge, we can move toward the path of healing by simply gaining new awareness. If every form of abuse distorts our sense of self and approach to others, we need to find out how that is playing out for us personally.

It starts with the courage to reflect, the willingness to be curious, and the resolve to truly understand your own story. After that, you share the story with your partner. You bring the same curiosity and attention to their story, offering them emotional presence and care. You look for echoes of those stories in the present.

For now, focus only on building awareness of where you've been. What is the story you lived? Go back to all the younger versions of you. What troubling emotions stand out? When were you conflicted, frustrated, or hurting? What left you feeling small, humiliated, or violated?

It is also helpful to consider what you have given to others but have not received yourself. We often are far better to our children and friends than we are to ourselves. It is crucial for you to see how, in the brilliance of your younger self, you survived the harm you endured. And you can grieve the harm you endured only to the degree that you approach the harm with a spirit of kindness.

Now is the time to fully accept your humanity. Acknowledge that you've known harm. Step into the "change agents" of humility and honesty. Sit with what rises in you.

All the while, remember this: You are more than your trauma. It doesn't get to name you.

And take heart, because your effort to gain awareness will ultimately take you somewhere new. You're addressing your past harm in order to manage it and keep it from bringing more present harm. You're positioning yourself for true healing and intimacy.

A Note from Becky

I t is amazing how easy it was to fall in love with Dan.

He was verbose and hilarious. Intense about loving Jesus and serious about his seminary training. Handsome and quick to take center stage in both my heart and with others.

At one point in our engagement, I broke up with him over theological differences, but it wasn't long before I was drawn back to him. As I watched him lead the singing of a hymn—with his terrible voice and an equally pathetic congregation—our differences became minimal. In that moment I fell in love again, because I realized he was a fool for Christ and I could trust his heart.

I felt far safer with him than I did with my family.

My mother was severe and rigid; I learned to stay out of her way, keep everything in its proper place, and never misbehave. It was clear who would win if I did. My parents were both productive leaders, enforcing their will in fierce, self-righteous ways. Weaponized authority and harsh language were the backdrop of my life.

Occasionally my father offered levity and warmth, and his tenderness was the balm I savored. He could tell incredible stories and delight in me. He also was prone to depression, and this was where I died a thousand deaths.

As I said, I did trust Dan's heart, but I wasn't quick to share my deepest hurts with him. I didn't want to bring anyone into those dark places. I didn't want to look at them at all.

In my senior year of high school, I dated a classmate who was manic-depressive. I adapted to his rhythms, tending to his sorrow and riding the waves of his mania, and endured his physical and sexual abuse. I broke up with him after a year, and he attempted suicide and went into a psychiatric ward. I returned to him. I broke up with him after a second year, and again, he attempted suicide and went to a different psychiatric ward. Again, I returned to him. I stayed for a third year, then finally left his bondage by transferring to a different university.

Abuse occurred again after my junior year of college, when I took part in an archaeological teaching session led by my academic adviser. A group of us camped out in the Rocky Mountains over six weeks, and on the last night, my professor came into my tent and raped me.

It wasn't until ten years into our marriage that I realized I needed care around my story. A colleague of Dan's, Pamela, became a safe place for me to reflect on my past. I told her things I'd never told anyone before.

"Becky, are you willing to tell Dan what you told me?" she asked.

I answered yes, then promptly avoided contact with her. I was so frightened.

Eventually Pamela facilitated a conversation with Dan and me when we all were at a hotel for a conference. She sat in our room and asked me to share with Dan. I was furious at these two professionals with their degrees, putting me in that position. I remained defiantly silent.

"If it takes hours until you're ready, that's fine," Pamela said. "I can miss my flight home for this."

The seriousness of her words struck me, and I started speaking—then hours ticked by like a speeding bullet train. It was a conversation that changed the course of my life and our marriage, setting us on a path of healing.

The word *trauma* was not a word I reckoned with until years later, when I went through the Allender Center training and allowed others to witness my story. It was hard, holy, and life-changing.

With others alongside me, I was able to grieve for the little girl who was scared to bother her mother and found refuge in closets.

For the twelve-year-old who developed asthma and didn't want to inconvenience her mother by not being able to breathe, who'd sooner faint than interrupt her.

For my younger self who, for twenty-four years, was prescribed night-time medication containing a stimulant, which made sleeping impossible for hours every night.

For the college student who was violated through physical and sexual violence.

For years, I didn't allow myself to look directly at my story. I'd instead look at my parents' traumas of being orphaned and hungry during the Great Depression and lose myself in looking at them. Or I'd see news reports of horrors like kidnapping and minimize my plight. Focusing only on myself seemed selfish.

But I now know that refusing to see the truth of my experiences is unkind. While my mother accomplished good things—raising funds for orphans and female college students—she didn't have her extravagant gaze on me. And there was harm in being so unseen.

Why didn't I feel safe enough to say, "Play with me; I want to be with you"?

Or, "I can't breathe. Help me"?

Or, "I can't sleep. Help me"?

Or, "My boyfriend is hurting me. I don't know what to do. Help me"?

Even now, it's still difficult for me to admit I've known trauma. On one hand, I know that is foolish. On the other, I don't want to admit I have scars.

I recently had surgery that left a protruding scar across my neck. I'm supposed to deep-massage the scar several times every day, but I dislike feeling it and tending to it. It'd be easier to wear turtlenecks for the rest of my life and hide the mark.

But I choose to tend to it because I want to heal.

I'm progressing in my climb of healing in my seventies. It is never too late to care for the body, soul, and heart.

It is never too late to become the person you're meant to be and to love your partner with more ferocity and joy.

It is never too late to tend to your trauma.

five

Looking at Your Operating System

Steve

With attentiveness, our inner worlds can become
beautiful and bountiful—not necessarily tame or
domesticated but abundantly fruitful and wildly alive.

LISA COLÓN DELAY

S ometimes I feel lonely when Kyle is away," my client Melissa said. "He's so often busy or traveling for work. There isn't much left for me."

Kyle sighed. "It's always the same story. She paints such a negative picture."

Melissa looked out the window. "Never mind. It doesn't matter."

Kyle shrugged and looked exhausted.

Deep heartache pulsated in every word and expression like an exposed nerve. A profound loneliness emanated from both of them.

"Let's shift gears a bit," I said. "Kyle, what was it like growing up in your family?"

"What does it matter? What's important about the past?" he asked, giving a response I hear often in therapy.

"The past actually plays a critical role in our present. We'll get to that, but for now, would you be willing to share a bit about some of the early experiences you remember, particularly with your mother or father?"

Kyle sighed and went silent. Then he said, "Well, my parents divorced when I was four, and I lived with my mom and younger brother. I lost contact with my dad within a few years. My mom really struggled after the divorce; she was gone a lot and was pretty distant when she was around." He paused, then began again. "I felt alone at home. So I focused on school and sports. I worked hard to stay out of trouble and get good grades, and I became the star quarterback."

As we continued to talk, it became clear that young Kyle had learned that his need to be comforted and soothed—particularly about his sadness over his father's abandonment—could not be met. This became part of the relational operating system he now has as adult Kyle. Today, he often dismisses any emotional need he has, which leaves his wife feeling alone and unimportant.

And this triggers her own trauma.

When I asked Melissa about her upbringing, she immediately teared up. "I was the youngest of three, and our parents left us alone for hours without supervision," she said. "We didn't have much. My mom often gave us food that was stale or even rotten and told us we should be grateful we had anything. Both of my parents were cold and harsh. I spent a lot of time in my room playing make-believe with my puppets."

Young Melissa suffered from not receiving the physical and emotional care she needed from her parents. She coped by retreating, which shaped adult Melissa's relational operating system.

When Kyle was emotionally distant from Melissa and unaware of the pain and heartache she felt, a wedge came between them. Their disconnection intensified.

Melissa's struggle to endure Kyle's neglect had led to a sense of despair she knew well from childhood. She once again felt left alone.

And ironically, so did Kyle.

The Connection We're Made For

Our deepest longing is to be cared for. From the moment we are born, we are hardwired to seek and maintain the presence of a caregiver, to be nourished physically and emotionally. We need someone to be *attuned* to us, to respond to our emotional and physical needs.

If you had a caregiver who consistently responded to your needs as a child, you developed a sense of security and safety, a connection that soothed your distress, calmed your fears, and provided reassurance. You experienced attunement.

But if you're like me, and many people I know, your experience with a parent was something quite different. They were often unavailable, distracted, absent, or inconsistent, leaving you confused and disoriented, and you developed strategies to survive relationally. You experienced a lack of attunement.

Attune means to "bring into harmony."[1] It is the capacity to "tune into" another person, simply being aware of them and their feelings. It's communicating care to someone by offering your presence and focus. Listening. Letting them know you get it. Interacting in a way that reassures their heart that they are seen and cared for.

When an attuned caregiver responds to the distraught cries of a child, the child is soothed and comforted. If this happens consistently, a child's needs become less distressing for them.

When a caregiver is not attuned with a child and does not meet their needs, the child learns that communicating their anguish is unlikely to bring a response. They may come to believe, *No one is interested in meeting my needs. There is no one I can trust to nurture, protect, and care for me. Now I must find a way to cope.* When their own need rises in them, they bury it, desperate to avoid the painful neglect, or even aggravation, of their caregiver. Expressing their need to an unattuned caregiver becomes simply unbearable.

This dynamic was proven in a study called the Still Face Experiment conducted by Dr. Edward Tronick. A mother first interacts playfully with her infant, then turns away for a moment. When she returns, she addresses the infant with a blank, expressionless face. The infant quickly attempts to engage her mother. But the mother's still, emotionless visage persists, and the child becomes frustrated. She whines, then shouts, trying to bring back the mother's engagement. Eventually, the baby begins wailing and writhing, wanting to escape her mother's blank expression; the child is in utter despair. When the mother suddenly responds and reengages, however, the child is soothed and calmed.[2]

This is a picture of human nature. Even as adults, we can see our relational DNA in this exchange and how it illustrates our critical need for attunement in every stage of life. As a child, when we can't get our parent to give us what we need, we withdraw and shut down, eventually escaping physically and within ourselves. As adults, when we reach out for connection with our spouses and the need is ignored or dismissed, our distress may feel similar to that childhood experience, even unbearable. We want to run and hide. We want to let out a visceral yell or hurl a plate at a wall or attack our spouses in some way—anything to release some of our anguish and evoke a response.

Attunement Trauma

My life began as an unplanned pregnancy for my mother. If she ever wanted children, it certainly wasn't at age twenty. She and my father got married to avoid scorn and judgment from family members, and they never became a couple who thrived.

My military father was frequently deployed overseas, and when he was home, he was still distant. He worked long hours and long days, often leaving at 6:00 A.M. and returning home at 6:00 P.M. On the weekends, he was typically busy with projects, and, consequently, gave us very little presence or emotional engagement.

My mother also struggled to be emotionally present, especially when my father was overseas. Our family life was terribly disrupted by his numerous moves, and conflict and tension at home became constant. My mother was often anxious, worried, and preoccupied; something else seemed more important than her children.

As my mother failed to meet my relational needs, I locked them down; it was too difficult and painful to hope for anything different. So I developed strategies to cope with the attunement that was missing. I'd escape to go fishing at a nearby lake or explore the woods to find comfort and peace alone. I'd seek attunement with neighborhood friends. But what I did most frequently might surprise you: I became for my mother what she wasn't for me. As the oldest child, I became a surrogate partner to her. I learned at a young age how to be attuned to my mother's needs, and when I was, I felt seen and like I mattered.

And this created in me an operating system I brought into my marriage.

Again, it comes back to that inner dialogue: No one is interested in meeting my needs. There is no one I can trust to nurture, protect, and care for me. Now I must find a way to cope.

This is *attunement trauma*—and yes, it is indeed trauma, even though it is not abuse or severe neglect. It's a relational wound that leaves us confused, overwhelmed, or uncertain where or how to find comfort. It's a result of ongoing unmet needs, and it steers us into a relational pattern that implies intimate relationships are unsafe and unpredictable.

Psychologist John Bowlby developed the idea of "internal working models": relational operating systems that our early interactions form in us. We all are "wired" by these lessons; they dictate our assumptions and expectations about how relationships work.[3]

In marriage, our spouses become our new attachment figures, and, although we're no longer children, we still seek—or avoid—relational connection in the same kinds of ways. What we couldn't make sense of in our parents in the past creates a similar discomfort and distress in us in the present.

The Familiar Song and Dance

It took nearly twenty-five years into my marriage for me to finally become aware of my early attunement trauma and why it created such a challenge for my wife, Lisa. I tended to withdraw and isolate whenever I felt emotionally disconnected from her, and this would, in turn, trigger Lisa's own attunement trauma story of profound loneliness.

This was our core relational pattern for over two decades, causing tremendous distress. Who had started it? We couldn't know. Who could end it? Neither of us. (Or, at least, it felt that way.)

As we both became preoccupied with life's many demands, the old feelings from our upbringings would crop up again, and, while it was very painful, it felt familiar. Lisa was again alone and neglected, and I was again an inconvenience and unimportant. It seemed reasonable to us both not to expect someone to want to connect or see us. So, we'd disengage and self-protect.

The lack of attunement in our relationship set in motion a deep feeling of loneliness from the past. It triggered our well-practiced survival strategies too. Even as the particular distress we felt as children was distant, our bodies, unconscious minds, and hearts remembered the old wounding and coping. We instinctively dismissed the need for connection and intimacy, convincing ourselves our needs were not important.

Lisa's mother was often emotionally unavailable and aloof toward Lisa as a child; having her emotional needs met by her mother seemed impossible. She learned at an early age, *Do not have emotional needs.* It was a message Lisa internalized deeply.

Lisa and I share a similar beginning to life. Lisa's mother was also pregnant before marriage, and her parents married three months into her mother's pregnancy. Throughout Lisa's early years, her mother was often unavailable emotionally, which set into motion a behavioral pattern many of us can relate to: *Work hard to hide any emotional need. Do not need comfort.* She learned to keep quiet, to be a good girl, and not to fuss or cry.

As a result, Lisa often missed the attunement her body craved. Attunement soothes us, and when it is not offered, especially early in life, our bodies learn to shut it down. The effect can be a profound sense of loneliness, and this was true for Lisa.

Today, the loneliness can creep in for her, especially when I am misattuned to her. She and I have recently become empty nesters and, while it's a new way of life I easily delight in, it has been a hard transition for Lisa. She misses having children in our home. A few days ago, she woke up feeling sad and attempted to communicate her feelings to me, seeking attunement. I, unfortunately, brushed it off.

"Really? You are still feeling sad?" I questioned coldly.

Lisa had allowed me to see her sensitive feelings and her need for care, and when she'd been hoping to receive comfort, she was met with judgment—the very thing we all are terrified of when we're vulnerable.

When I responded harshly, Lisa's attunement trauma came back to her. She felt confused and disoriented. *Why is my husband not responding to me in a way that cares for me or soothes me?* Not being able to receive comfort from a spouse always prompts this feeling; we can't make sense of what is happening. Typically, Lisa ultimately interprets it as reaffirming that she should not need. I do the same, and it is because we both come from childhoods that taught us, *It is safest not to need.*

This has been our song and dance for decades: the war against need. It has been the leading cause of disconnection in our marriage. We've had to learn new inner dialogues: *It is normal to need. It is healthy to reach for emotional connection. I will not retreat; I will keep my heart open.*

I've seen others with past attunement trauma create a dynamic in their marriage that is entirely based on what their spouse needs. They prioritize the other person from an intense desire for connection. They become preoccupied with learning to attune to their spouse's needs, hoping their spouse will turn toward them. It's a sense of "look at me" or "watch"—a childlike behavior tied to an adult who deeply needs to be seen, noticed, and responded to.

Again, the answer is not to deny or bury our needs; they are part of our humanity. But our reactions to them and the ways we handle them—that we can change. Operating systems formed by our past can be re-formed today.

We do that by addressing them so we can begin to understand them.

Look for Patterns

Attunement trauma can be so subtle that it is often ignored, minimized, or dismissed. When it goes unaddressed, it can become the undercurrent that keeps couples apart. They usually aren't even aware of the source and feel bewilderingly stuck in their emotional distance.

If you find yourself in this place, take heart that many have been where you are and have moved forward in a new direction. Consider a few things you can do now to help make that shift.

The first and most difficult step is, of course, reflecting on your formative childhood moments. If you and I were sitting together, I might ask you what I asked Kyle and Melissa: "Would you be willing to share a bit about some of the early experiences you remember, particularly with your mother or father?" Consider how you'd answer, especially how you did or did not feel seen and cared for, and how you responded.

As you look back, be gentle with yourself. Try to release any shame over your wounding and coping. What you did when you were young to survive was brilliant and beautiful. It enabled you to live with fewer wounds when there was little capacity to choose another direction. Allow yourself to accept and respect this.

Also acknowledge, however, that those survival techniques were for another time, and that using them today will undoubtedly move you away from a flourishing life. Aim to understand what compelled the younger you to defend yourself while also opening yourself to other ways of addressing past and present harm now.

Next, start to pay attention to your frequent thoughts and reactions to difficult moments. What patterns do you find? How might they mirror your behavior in earlier years?

I recently returned home earlier than expected from one of my fly-fishing trips with Dan. Lisa had invited friends to spend the weekend in our home while I was away, so that's what I came back to. Time with friends, of course, brings her such delight—to be seen and known, to feel connected and loved. There is a redemptive quality for her in experiencing attunement from other women, particularly because of what wasn't true in her relationship with her mother. I know this and I support this, 100 percent.

And yet, as I walked through the kitchen and saw the delight on Lisa's face from being with such good friends, there was an old heavy feeling that flashed in me and lingered. An imprint of attunement trauma. I had the familiar thought, *She would rather be with others than be with me*—it's a thought I'd had countless times about my mother.

What we remember as adults is not often a vivid, conscious memory. It is simply felt. I felt lonely for a few minutes. I felt unimportant for a few minutes. My body reacted and responded to my relational story of "something else is always more important." It's a common type of experience for any of us who endured a lack of attunement in our early years of development.

Like I said, these emotions stayed with me for a few minutes, but it easily could have been longer. A previous version of me would have rushed to my office, crumbling and fuming, and camped out there for hours, emerging with only coldness toward Lisa. A couple things kept me from spiraling this time.

I had become aware of my tendencies. When that feeling flashed and that thought rushed in, I could identify, *There's that familiar reaction. Yep, that is my instinct.* And then I could think, *But I am not with my distant mother. Look at what is real in this moment. I am tied to my loving wife.*

I also had been making an effort to foster attunement with Lisa. I could recall recent moments of connection to reassure myself that I mattered to her and anticipate future moments of connection. I could process that seeing Lisa enjoy time with others didn't mean she no longer wanted to be close to me. The attunement between us prevented a reactivation of the same distress I'd known in the past.

Let's return to Kyle and Melissa, the couple from the beginning of this chapter. I spent a few more sessions with them processing how the lack of attunement they experienced in their upbringing was impacting their dynamic. The key to any change in marriage is awareness. Once Kyle and Melissa became more aware of how their collective attunement trauma was impacting their relationship, they began to develop new ways of responding to each other. Kyle learned to be emotionally present more consistently. Melissa became more emotionally available to Kyle. They offered access to each other, which became a healing balm and a redemptive experience for them both. Their newfound attunement was cultivating soil that had become hardened and seemingly impenetrable over many years.

So consider your own story. Think about what you faced as a child and how you responded. See how it might be playing out now. What is your body remembering and carrying? What instincts are still part of you? Did you often have an inner dialogue as a child, perhaps even subconsciously, that still feels familiar today?

Gently notice without judgment. And if judgments arise, can you, for a moment, tend to them without agreement or an effort to banish them? Simply observe all you can and gather the information, knowing it is part of positioning yourself to walk a different path. Learn your current operating system, be open to adopting new relational patterns, and you will be able to start moving toward powerful attunement and intimacy with your partner.

Part Two

Disrupting Divisive Patterns and Changing the Atmosphere

Creating Safety When Feeling Threatened

Dan

Be kind to each other, tenderhearted, forgiving one another, just as God through Christ has forgiven you.

EPHESIANS 4:32 NLT

It could be said that I am the computer expert in our marriage. But that's like saying a student who got a score of twenty out of a hundred on a test is twice as proficient in the topic as someone who got a ten. Becky and I are both incompetent, but I occasionally stumble toward a few solutions that befuddle her.

One day as I was working in our living room, Becky walked toward me with her laptop, looking anxious and forlorn. As she sat next to me, my body tensed and stiffened. Given her expression and the presence of her laptop, I knew the coming moments would be unpleasant and frustrating. Plus, she was disrupting my focus. *Doesn't she recognize that I'm working? She wouldn't barge into my office, but because I'm on the couch, she thinks I'm interruptible.*

From this defensive state, I engaged with her.

Becky: I don't understand why this email keeps showing up, saying we don't have sufficient funds in our checking account. I know we do, but it says I need to rectify a problem with our account.

Dan: It's likely phishing. You didn't click on any website in the email, did you?

Becky: I don't remember if I did or not.

Dan: *What?* I've told you a thousand times—when something in an email doesn't make sense, or if there is a document to open, you must check who sent it.

Becky: Stop it. You're angry. Even if I made a mistake, which I'm not sure I did, I don't need your contempt.

Dan: Do you understand your computer and our bank account might have been compromised, and if that is the case, we have hours ahead of changing passcodes and checking with our bank?

Becky: I know it's a big deal, but I don't need you making me feel like a fool.

Dan: Fine. If you screwed up, then it's up to you to fix it. I don't have the time.

Becky: Go do your important work. I'll figure it out.

This interchange breaks my heart as I recall it. It didn't when it was occurring or immediately afterward; it took me ninety minutes to admit I'd failed. I'd hurt Becky. I'd replicated past harm in our marriage. And I'd reinforced patterns she'd suffered with her mom.

I did this in reaction to being triggered (which I'll soon explain). Regardless, Becky came to me expecting safety, support, and partnership, and instead was met with resistance, exasperation, and criticism.

To address the regular issues of life—problems, decisions, conflicts, hurts—with a spouse in a healthy way, both hearts must feel free to engage them without judgment or punishment. If one or both feel unsafe, some kind of relational fallout is inevitable, even if an issue is resolved quickly. Somewhere down the line, the pattern will repeat, and the buried buildup of hurts from past unsafe moments will rise to the surface.

To steer ourselves away from that perpetual hurt and division, we need to be more intentional about offering each other kindness and respect in those moments, looking for ways to make room for connectedness and care.

We need to create space for safety.

To do this, we must first understand what is making us feel unsafe and how we're reacting to it.

Our Brains on Threat

When Becky came to me needing help, my bristly response created an atmosphere where she felt vulnerable to attack. Feeling a lack of safety always means we are facing a threat, perhaps of shame, loss, or trauma, and we can't experience that without particular things happening inside us, things that are outside the norm of day-to-day life.

Sensing a threat affects every part of our being—our bodies, brains, hearts, and spirits. Its impact is comprehensive and complex, changing our ability to relate to ourselves, others, and God. It is a shock to our system, one we are wired to react to it instantaneously in biological, psychological, and relational ways: we fragment, we numb, and we isolate.

Fragmenting

Fragmenting means, in a sense, that we are falling apart. The brain takes a break from its standard operating mode as one of its critical components checks out.

The left hemisphere of the brain manages our thoughts, reasoning, deduction, and choices; the right hemisphere controls our feelings, impulses, images, and sensations. When we feel a threat to our existence, part of the left hemisphere goes offline. It is not that all our executive functioning is shut off like a light switch; it is more like a dimmer switch that goes from bright to dim instantly.[1] As a result, instead of reasoning, we react emotionally.

Fragmentation of thought *protects us* from the slowness of cerebral deliberation and *frees us* to simply run with the faster, emotional-decision-making part of our brains.

While reactivity helps us in moments of physical danger (say, if a tiger were chasing us), it can perpetuate harm in moments of relational tension. This is because our reactivity is often broken; it was formed by the ways we reacted to trauma in the past. Suppose early in our neurological mapping of reality, we experienced a threat of being shamed for making a mistake and learned that turning away from the criticism allowed us to mitigate the internal upheaval. This then became our default mechanism, and, decades later, we're still doing it.

Sensing a threat not only prompts part of the left hemisphere to go offline but also triggers our stress systems to go rapidly online.

Our amygdalae secrete biochemicals that activate us to deal with the threat. As they pulse through our brains, we lose a sense of time—the past, the future, even the progression of present moments. We focus on a narrow band of reality and lose the ability to consider the complexity and context of our current plights.

We are merely trying to survive. And our thoughts are a scramble.

This is what happens when we feel stunned and speechless, lose our tempers and yell, or snap an insult in retaliation.

It also can look less dramatic. After a friend told me about his bleak medical diagnosis over the phone, I ended the call and couldn't remember what I'd been doing beforehand. I wandered the house, started working on an unfinished task, stopped to open mail, then picked up my phone but forgot what I was going to do. I was fragmenting. It was only when I sat down and began to feel the weight of the news and own what I felt that my rational thinking came back online.

Numbing

Fragmenting leads to numbing, when something in our bodies says, *I can't bear this*. We cannot become aware of the extent of the anger, grief, or fear in us—it is too much. Subconsciously we sense the danger of, *What if I physically harm someone in anger, or I never stop crying in my grief, or my panic puts me in the hospital?* It's better to just *push it down*. This is how we survive.

When this happens amid a threat, the parasympathetic nervous system (PSNS) slows down the body and numbs our emotions to regulate their intensity. The body and brain work to limit the liability of feelings that could lead us away from safety.

After the phone call from my friend who shared bad news, I not only fragmented but also became numb. I didn't want to feel the fear and threat he was experiencing, so I got busy, even if I couldn't remember what I was trying to accomplish. Going numb gives us a small space of time to not feel out of control and to establish some grounding before the next wave crashes. Eventually, after wandering around the house, it was time for me to stop and feel.

Isolating

The third thing that happens in our automatic threat response is disconnecting, both internally and relationally. We create demilitarized zones that separate us from the harm and give us ground to return to ourselves.[2]

Becky isolates by cleaning the house. I isolate by reading. Others might finish a project, slam a door, text a friend, or watch Instagram reels for an hour to regulate their stress response.

Typically, an hour or a day later, we return to each other. We may acknowledge failures and forgiveness, but the DMZ between us is never truly entered; that space becomes the ground where foul fruit grows. The cycle of perceiving threats, fragmenting, numbing, and isolating goes on, and the roots of our trauma responses are not addressed.

To engage the roots, we must examine the ground of our families of origin.

I shared with you in chapter 2 that my mentally ill mother had been extremely dependent on me, and that Becky's independence drew me in. She would resolve her struggles on her own rather than turning to me. I didn't feel the burden of handling her angst the way I had with my mother, who relied on me to keep her from plunging into the abyss of her insecurities. I saw Becky as the perfect partner who wanted to be with me but, mercifully, didn't need me.

Becky, however, behaved this way as a result of her own trauma. She had learned it was dangerous to have a need or desire that aggravated her mother. As a child she coped by hiding in closets to distance herself from her mother's fury. Becky formed the habit of metabolizing her mom's rage by being silent and invisible. I saw a desirable stability in her, not knowing that it was born out of a deep refusal to need.

We were a perfect pair: I am intense and (often) angry, and Becky is calming and (often) kind.

And so, when Becky came to me desperate for help with her laptop, she triggered me on two levels: I'm not used to her being needy, and I hate feeling incompetent. Computers are diabolic instruments that we must use but are created to frustrate us. And technical problems often lead to the torture of dealing with either a nonsensical bot or an infinitely delayed person in customer service. All of this boiled up inside me when she asked for help.

As each of us fragmented, I exploded, and she retaliated.

Then we both went numb and isolated from each other.

High-Alert Habits

There are a few other ways we can understand how we react to threats: we flee, fight, freeze, and fawn. These are expressions of what we've discussed earlier. When we begin to fragment, it unnerves us; we feel flustered and try to escape (flight) or get angry (fight) and try to gain control. We're examining that same automatic reactivity here but looking at it in different categories of external responses to the internal effects of trauma. We all utilize all four responses, but we learn to depend on one more than the others over time.

As you read through these, remember: (1) the brain is constantly scanning the world for potential dangers, standing ready to release stress biochemicals like adrenaline and cortisol to enable us to handle them, and (2) our response to any perceived threat is not a thinking choice but a visceral, embodied, adaptive reaction.

Anxiety and Flight

Becky is prone to feeling anxiety and fear in the face of danger more than I am; it is impossible to know to what degree this is due to genetics or learning.[3] In any case, her frequent response is fleeing, turning to other activities that help reorder her external and internal worlds. She turns away from the threat by doing a solitary, productive activity like cleaning, something that gives her some control.

I've often found her pattern of moving away cowardly and disingenuous. *Stand your ground, girl, and let's get this problem resolved,* I'd mentally insist. The more she'd move away, the more I'd foam and fume.

I am more aligned with anger.

Anger and Fight

While the primary response to threats is anxiety, anxiety can fuse with a sense of injustice (*This is wrong and should not be*). That's when anger rises. Anger is anxiety mobilized to face a foe, activating our will to overpower or intimidate the threat.

No one is born angry, but we are in the womb with a fully formed amygdala that generates anxiety. We experience pain as infants, and our cries express fear and frustration. Both emotions signal a need for care, for someone to offer comfort and sustenance to lessen our suffering.

As we age, our fear and frustration are socially disruptive, so parents and schools work vigorously to limit, mollify, or shame them. An angry child is sent to the hallway. An anxious child is told to buck up and get it together. Providing space to engage with the threat these emotions are reacting to is time-consuming and considered impractical. Culturally, we have few resources to address fear or anger, especially trauma-related ones.

As I've said, when I feel a threat, my first reaction is usually anger. Growing up, tuning into my anger kept me from tuning into the despair and shame that haunted our house like a phantom. My raging temper tantrums became the focal point of my emotionally chaotic mother and my passive, disengaged father, and, oddly, this brought them solace and strength. My anger was like a charge that dissipated the ion-filled anxiety pervading our world and somehow soothed us all.

It is imperative to note that the threat was just as real and the core anxiety just as present in my home as in Becky's. The difference is that "acting out" in a way that would dissipate the family's awareness of the anxiety was an option in my world and not in hers. We each are a complex mosaic comprising the same tiles but in vastly different trauma configurations.

Given our tendencies shaped by our upbringings, when Becky and I have conflict, I often move against her, and she moves away from me. The further I move against her, the more she leaves. The more she departs, the more I am apt to bluster. It is a self- and couple-defeating cycle. But in the moment, it feels more reasonable and life-protecting than any other response in heaven or on earth.

Avoidance and Freezing or Fawning

When we suddenly encounter something terrible, we often can't speak or move and may even faint. We cope by dissociating.

Becky once called me at a conference to tell me that a dear friend had died by suicide. As I heard the words, a sickening horror swept over me like a rogue wave, then I collapsed. I became aware that I'd moved only after hearing Becky's frantic voice from the fallen phone.

We freeze when a threat radically overwhelms our neural pathways, like an electric charge shorting out a fuse. It is a shutting down of thought and feeling, an escape from danger by disconnecting from reality. Freezing can be momentary, last for hours, or, at its extreme, move into a kind of fugue state of catatonia.

Another form of avoidance is fawning—resolving tension by stifling emotion, pleasing others, and eating the problem rather than addressing it. Fawning is also called *chronic compromise*, or letting others make decisions. It usually involves camouflaging ourselves to escape notice.

One friend of mine constantly has a smile on her face. She is an upbeat, warm human being, but her smile originated in her childhood as a younger sister to two brothers—one who was autistic, and one who was sexually abusive. Her dad was physically absent; her mother was emotionally absent. She lived in a war zone, and her smile protected her from the horror.

As an adult, she's still in the habit of fawning. It is not insincere or manipulative, but a biological means to manage internal and external chaos by doing whatever seems to keep other people happy.

Freezing is neither moving away nor against; it is leaving all movement to the one perceived as the threat.

Fawning is a movement toward the threat; it appears to offer relationship but is primarily avoiding more danger by doing whatever it takes to defuse the conflict.

Developing Safety

Constantly reacting to threats will never increase intimacy or move us toward health and maturity. Any marriage that lacks safety has not developed sufficient trust to do the hard work of growing together.

So how do we begin to create safety and build trust?

First, we become aware of the perceived threats in our relationship and our reactions to them.[4] Then, we pay close attention when it is happening and work to manage ourselves in new ways. We learn to push out any possibility of more harm and make room for respectful awareness of our spouses.

The Wisdom of Pausing

This is no small feat. Our automatic reactions to threats involve rapid-fire neurological processes that outpace our capacity for rational, left-brain resolve. We can't reverse the process because our stress biochemicals are crashing on the shore of our brains.

What we can do, however, is *stop*.

As impossible as that sounds, we are indeed able to stop the rampage and the additional harm it will bring. What is needed is space, a time to pause.

This only can happen if you recognize the signs of a threat response. Can you feel your body ramp up? Do you notice your pulse quicken, your breath shorten, your heart beat faster? It also requires the humility to admit you are feeling triggered, and your body is near to, or already, being hijacked.

For some spouses who hate conflict, this will come with an increase of fear. For others, it will be accompanied by a surge of anger and arousal. When we feel activated and the rising necessity to flee, fight, freeze, or fawn, *it is time to stop*.[5]

Even if we can justify our reaction of running away or digging in our heels, we must let that go. Only then can we ask our partners for a pause so we can collect ourselves (care for fragmentation), tend to our emotions (tend to numbness), and make a decision not to isolate.

The Perspective of Story

There is something else we must do to give ourselves space to restore and return to each other, and it is far more complex than a simple technique: *we must be caught more deeply in the realm of story than in the moment of threat.* We can't create space for restoration for our partners or ourselves unless we know the core stories of heartache and harm from both of our lives.

At first, this will sound like a left-brain, logical attempt to calm a right-brain, emotional storm—which never works. The only way to regulate a supercharged amygdala is through reaching that *feeling* part of the brain, and that's what *true knowing* does. It involves right-brain activity as we reenter the stories that have shaped us. We reflect and imagine; we feel and suffer.

True knowing begins by naming how we handled threats before we met our spouses. We must become embedded in both of our past contexts—the characters, plots, dialogues, and outcomes—to actually feel those experiences and taste their bitter fruit. Then we can begin the process of owning how our past harm triggers the warfare of our spouses.

The choice to pause is not a one-and-done labor. We will need to keep reentering those stories with greater depth and insight over multiple reiterations. We must commit to knowing our own young, broken parts as well as our partners'. Anything less will be a failure of care and lead to less safety and trust.

Once when Becky and I were preparing to go to a wedding, she asked me, "What are you wearing tonight?"

I looked at her like she'd fallen off her rocker. "A suit. My only suit. My blue suit."

"If you wear that and I wear the blue dress I planned to wear, we'll look like we're wearing identical bowling shirts."

I laughed and said, "I don't have another suit."

She scrunched her nose and shrugged, and we were at an impasse.

I could leave her disappointed, simply acquiesce, or create safety with her. If all we wanted to do was be on the same page, I could have resolved the conflict quickly by forgoing the suit and choosing a sport coat and a nice pair of pants instead. But there was more in this moment to address. We needed to take the time to pause and account for our history of handling tension and conflict.

"Come, let's sit down and talk," I said. "You have a beautiful blue dress, and I want you to wear it. And apparently, you seem to fear anyone knowing we like to bowl."

She smiled. The offer to slow down and not "decide" but just talk seemed to lighten the mood. Even my small attempt at humor let in some warmth.

"I don't fully understand your concern, but I'm not dismissing it," I assured her. "I can wear something different. But what's most important to me is hearing what triggered such a strong reaction to matching colors."

Becky, who grew up as a stockbroker's daughter, began to tell me what it was like to go to high-profile events with her mother's nightmarish pressure to look perfect. She'd quickly be on the receiving end of her mother's rage at the slightest flaw or misstep. The issue of my suit and her dress had nothing to do with the fear of matching colors; it had gotten tangled in the web of fear and humiliation from her past.

When we see anxiety, anger, or avoidance surface, we must open the door to what those emotions are telling us about our unaddressed trauma. We need to create safety and room for our stories to unfold and for our hearts to connect.

A Different Script

What if, when Becky had come to me with her computer, we had chosen to create space for safety?

If I had known I was being triggered, I could have said, "Give me a minute. I feel a lot right now and don't want to let it spill out on you."

By setting the parameters of what I didn't want to do *in light of who I wanted to be*, I'd be able to return to something more profound than the current problem or past trauma. Doing this sets the intention in the face of the storm and then steadies the compass before choosing to move.

If I had given myself time, it wouldn't have taken me long to see how Becky's desperation pulled up in me what I had felt with my mother. That reality alone would have given me pause, grief, and *a heightened intention not to replicate what I often did when I felt threatened.*

By no means am I implying this is easy; it is not. But on the other hand, it is simple. I needed to create space for us to first address not how to resolve the problem but *how we wanted to be* in the interaction.

When Becky explained her problem to me, I could have said:

Dan: Oh no. It's so frustrating to be caught in that maze. Before we start problem-solving, I'll acknowledge that, in the past, I've not handled these kinds of moments with you and the computer well. I want you to know I am for you, and we are together in this.

Becky: Thank you. Yes, I clearly remember how this has not gone well before. I was anxious about bringing this up to you, but I just can't figure it out on my own.

Dan: Well, we both know this is an issue that has provoked us. Let's keep close to the bone and be quick to address either your anxiety or my anger so we don't repeat what we've often done.

Attunement and creating space for a safe interaction slows our brains, orients us in our story, and gives us perspective on our problems. It gives us more access to the roots of what is triggering us and more ground to grow good fruit.

So the next time your pulse quickens in a moment of tension, pause. When your brain jumps to a familiar survival reaction with your spouse, stop. Give yourself a minute. Notice your instinctive responses and what you're reacting to.

Remind yourself there could be another way.

Slowly consider the roots and the bigger story, for both you and your spouse.

And then reengage with patience and gentle consideration.

Quieting the Whisper of Shame

Steve

Shame is the lie that someone told you about yourself.

A. KIN

Your birthday's coming up. Do you want to have a party here at the house? You could invite friends—just a few."

My mother's words stopped me in my tracks, thrilled me, then sent my second-grade brain racing. She rarely thought about what I might need or want and then followed through with it. Given that history of negligence, could I trust her to do this for me? I had to choose to take her at her word or ignore my core desire to be celebrated by my friends and honored by my mother, to feel their warm acceptance and love deep down in my gut.

My desire won out.

What I'd imagined, however, did not end up happening. While my mother did indeed host a party, she exuded annoyance and drudgery, never joy and excitement. "Why did I say this was a good idea? It's so much work!" she complained. Opening presents was a chore. Cutting and serving the cake was stressful. Clearly, she was fulfilling an obligation, not genuinely celebrating her son; the whole ordeal was a bother.

As soon as our last guest left, my mother announced, "We aren't doing that again," with obvious disdain.

And deep in my heart, a new emotion joined my desire: shame.

I am a fool to trust. I am a fool to need. I stupidly put myself in an unsafe place.

I had prioritized my desire, accepting the risk involved, and this is where I wound up.

Maybe when you read the word *shame* above, you thought, *Nope, I'm out. Not going to go there.* Trust me, I understand. But I want to encourage you to linger here a bit even as it's uncomfortable.

The truth is, there is no shame in feeling shame. It is part of the human experience. And when we are willing to be curious about it, we often find it is covering a real need that has gone unmet or a wound that has not yet healed. We also might see how it's perpetuating more and more hurt, which we can disrupt. Eventually, we can gain the ability to overcome it and build resilience to it. But to do that, we must come to really understand our experience of it.

What Exactly Is Shame?

It is easy to confuse shame with guilt. Guilt is when *I feel bad* for what I've done, thought, or felt. Shame is the sense that *I am bad* for what I've done, thought, or felt. Sometimes we feel bad about what we've done, which is natural, and it can motivate us to do something different.

One day Lisa and I were looking for a parking space outside a grocery store, and I pulled into a fifteen-minute spot. Lisa gave me a sideways glance that said, *Really? Is this a good choice?* We both knew our shopping

QUIETING THE WHISPER OF SHAME

would take longer than fifteen minutes. I felt bad about *doing* something wrong, so I pulled out of the spot and found another one. Guilt can help us make a different choice.

Shame, at its root, is judgment against ourselves. According to psychiatrist Curt Thompson, shame is the feeling connected to the belief that there is "something wrong with me."[1]

We fear being exposed as "not okay" and being outright rejected. We don't want to reveal what we need, desire, or feel, because we are terrified our spouses will judge us and turn away from us; then we will be left feeling profoundly alone (which we will explore more in chapter 9). Brené Brown defines shame as "the intensely painful feeling or experience of believing that we are flawed and therefore unworthy of love and belonging."[2] Shame skews our view of our worth, isolates us, and inhibits us from experiencing what we deeply need and long for.

I have seen countless versions of this story of shame in therapy over the years. People spend years needing to be seen, known, and valued, to be noticed, celebrated, and cherished. But the loudest voice in their lives has been shame, saying, *You are not enough. You don't really belong with anyone. Your needs and hopes don't matter.*

Where does all of this come from? From early in our stories, from those formative moments when someone else's actions screamed, *You are not acceptable*—and we internalized it intensely. We believed it to our core.

Maybe it was the mother who couldn't "dial in" to our feelings. The father who issued one judgment after another. A coach who criticized us in the presence of others. A music teacher complaining that we were always off key. The emotional neglect that left us feeling alone in our rooms, the trauma of our sexual abuse, or the physical violence we experienced from a family member.

We all experience trauma, and shame always accompanies relational trauma.

It then wriggles into our sense of self and our operating system. We follow *shame scripts* in our thoughts—repeatedly telling ourselves who we are through the lens of judgment. These internal scripts guide us through our relational world and influence us in "how to be" with our spouses.

We typically do all this without being aware of it. So let's look closer at some of the lies shame whispers to us and how we accept them and run with them.

"Your Feelings Are Not Seen or Valid"

In chapter 5, we discussed the critical experience of attunement, when someone tunes into another person. We all are wired to receive this; *it is a legitimate human need*. We all need someone to offer us their presence and focus, to show they are aware of our feelings, to listen and empathize, and to reassure our hearts that we are seen and cared for.

The lack of attunement is usually where shame develops. It is a form of emotional neglect, which is a form of trauma.

This was the case for Melissa, whom we met in chapter 5. When she was young, she struggled to fall asleep, feeling anxious and afraid of the dark. She would secretly sneak into her parents' bedroom to avoid being alone, and her mother would respond with ridicule and criticism.

"What's wrong with you?" she'd say. "There's nothing to be afraid of! Go back to your room." Any chance of Melissa's need for comfort and soothing being met was off-limits; the needs themselves were deemed unacceptable.

When Melissa was an older child, whenever her mother saw her daughter in tears about something, she would turn away from Melissa—often going into her room and closing the door. *What's wrong with me?* Melissa wondered. *Why won't my mother comfort me?* The only way she could make sense of her mother's response was, once again, to conclude, *I am the problem. Something is wrong with me and my need to be comforted.*

Her mother consistently could not attune with Melissa—could not dial in to what she needed—and Melissa developed an embedded shame narrative. *I'm not important. I don't matter.*

When our parents do not offer attunement, we receive it as a form of judgment. *Your need is too much. Your need is not okay.* Receiving judgment from those who are meant to love, soothe, and nurture us contributes to the shame we feel—and to the shame scripts we start living with.

So years later, when adult Melissa experienced distance from her husband, she fell into the same deep shame she had felt when her mother pushed her away. As Kyle was frequently preoccupied with work and unavailable to Melissa, sometimes for days at a time, he was unattuned and unable to respond to her needs. She occasionally sensed judgment from him about her needs. And her internal script laced with judgment would say, *What's wrong with you? Quit being upset. You don't deserve more time with your husband.*

"You Must Not Need"

I can relate to Melissa. With an emotionally unavailable mother, I internalized many negative messages about my value and learned to squash down my needs to survive. And the old shame I felt as a child can rise in me as an adult. It can show up in the simplest everyday moments.

Lisa and I recently went to our favorite Italian restaurant to celebrate her birthday, and when we arrived, the hostess walked us to a table at the very back of the restaurant near the noisy kitchen. All my excitement for this chance to honor Lisa deflated. Here we were in our nice clothes, feeling cramped and hearing hollers of "Table ten is ready!" I'd hoped for a quiet table by the front window with no distractions and a beautiful view. Before I knew it, I'd gone from bothered to irritated to upset.

Did I ask the hostess if it was possible to wait for another table near the front window? Sadly, no—I was entirely absorbed in my shame script. *Do not need, do not ask for anything, do not be an inconvenience.*

Then I was flooded with familiar messages, ones that hurt deeply, just as they had in the past: *It's not okay for you to need or desire something different. No one will accept your request.* And the kicker, *You don't deserve something better.*

As shame spun through me, I wasn't emotionally present with Lisa. I wanted to celebrate her and enjoy connection with her, but I got caught up in wrestling my desire for a different table and my sense of feeling small. The familiar angst of not being able to name what I needed and wanted took over, and I couldn't connect with Lisa.

We see here, as we will in other parts of this discussion, that *shame ultimately leads to disconnection.*

"Go Hide"

Shame's original meaning is *an attempt to cover oneself.*[3] When we feel shame, we want to cover ourselves or to hide.

Hiding was the core relational response of Adam and Eve in the garden of Eden. Once they realized that eating the forbidden fruit was a form of dishonor, they chose to *hide* from God among the trees. When God found them, Adam admitted, "I was afraid because I was naked; so I hid" (Genesis 3:10).

You and I do the same thing when we fear exposure and feel shame. We try to hide.

Exposure feels unbearable because we are overcome with our sense of inadequacy. We are terrified of being seen, because we are terrified of judgment. After all, our shame tells us we will be found unacceptable.

We may not hide behind trees like Adam and Eve did, but we find other ways to hide from each other.

The other day, Lisa and I sat together over coffee with the intention of bringing our full presence and focus to each other. We had only a few minutes to connect. Just after we sat down, though, our daughter in college called Lisa, and, to my surprise, Lisa answered it.

Notice here that shame can be sneaky and appear in the most benign moments; this was one of them for me.

As Lisa started chatting, I got up and left the room, stinging with disappointment and rejection. Shame seared me, murmuring, *You don't matter to her. She'd pick someone else over you in a heartbeat.* And even, *There is something fundamentally wrong with you.*

Intellectually, I knew that this wasn't true, but it honestly felt true. Sometimes shame can override all logic and reasoning. When we feel something, *it just feels true.*

To cope, I rushed to my den and put a basketball game on the TV as a distraction. I hid.

It was an attempt to seek safety. As one of my favorite musicians, Joshua Radin, wrote, "I've grown accustomed to safety by hiding."⁴ When we're afraid of what our spouses might think about us, we hide to avoid exposure. We want to *cover* ourselves. We believe hiding will temporarily relieve us from our shame and protect us from further judgment and ridicule.

This, I confess, is a frequent reaction for me when I feel shame. I tend to withdraw and go away.

A few years ago, I was coaching a high school boys' basketball team, and we were playing the biggest game of the season. Stakes were high as we faced a rival team after we'd trained hard for weeks—and my father was in the stands.

Devastatingly, we ended up losing, and I honestly wanted to run out of the gym. More than any other emotion, I felt shame. I wanted to cope by hiding, and I tried desperately to do so. As the team walked back to the locker room, I was silent. As we rode home on the bus, I sat away from my players. *Don't look at me when I don't measure up*, my shame said. *If you do, you will see just how deficient I am.* I kept seeing the disappointed eyes of my father that I took to mean, *How could you lose?* Notice the tone of judgment, even accusation, here.

I can tell you, based on therapy sessions with many folks, that this is a typical response when we feel shame. We try to escape because the exposure is just unbearable.

Here is the bind, though: withdrawing when we feel shame *creates more shame*. It grows exponentially in isolation. "We feel shame, and then feel shame for feeling shame," wrote Curt Thompson. "It begets itself."[5]

Let Yourself Be Found

We can respond to shame and find relief from it in a different way—a way that doesn't hurt ourselves, our partners, or our connection to each other. In fact, it brings healing. And this far better path begins with choosing to be *found* in our experience of shame.

Let's go back to the garden, when Adam and Eve were coping by hiding. How did our Father God handle seeing his dear ones consumed with shame?

He pursued them.

"Where are you?" he called, though he knew exactly where they were. His question was out of desire and out of love. He wanted them to *feel pursued*. It is a beautiful portrayal of what we are invited to do with his Spirit in response to our spouses' shame. *I know you long to be seen and loved. I will see and love you.*

Can you imagine offering this to your spouse when they seem to feel shame? Can you imagine receiving it from them when you feel it?

Some clients I've worked with can't help but interpret a question like *Where are you?* from their partner as a judgment or accusation. But what we are discussing here is truly a curiosity driven by desire, an expression of a pursuing love.

If we are the ones pursuing our partners, we can explore a number of ways we can convey to our spouses, *I am here and I care. I want to be with you and comfort you.*

Curiosity

I have found that one of the most helpful ways to engage someone feeling shame is through openhearted curiosity.

When Lisa and I were at the noisy restaurant table, and I was convincing myself "not to need" and recounting how little I deserved in life, Lisa noticed something was off. Clearly, I had gone offline. Kindly she asked, "Hey, where are you?" Her curiosity loosened the grip of shame in me.

In other scenarios, curiosity in response to our spouses' shame may sound like, "What happened? You seem a bit distracted. Want to check in about it?"

Curiosity is an invitation and not a requirement. It opens a door and invites our spouses in. It communicates, *I want to care for you*, and makes room for our spouses to share what they are feeling. Curiosity helps us tell the story of what happened, and, as Ann Voskamp once wrote, "Shame dies when we tell stories in safe places."[6] Curiosity is foundational to safety.

Empathy

When our partners feel shame, they need to receive empathy. Empathy loosens the grip of shame.

As I was returning home from my epic failure coaching the basketball game, I just wanted to be left alone (I'm owning the pattern). Lisa knew we had lost. When she heard me come through the door, she greeted me and immediately could see how wretched I felt.

"Oh Steve, I'm so sorry. I know you're crushed. It's hitting you deeply—of course it is. I get how this might fuel shame for you too. It's so hard; it just feels awful."

This is how empathy looks and sounds, and it was exactly what I needed. Here was a reminder that I wasn't alone, I was seen and found, and my wife deeply loved me, even though my shame script was so loud.

Brené Brown once said, "Shame cannot survive when met by empathy."[7] Empathy is the antidote to shame. It says to our spouses, *I get it, and I'm here with you.*

Life-Giving Truth-Telling

When we are in the throes of shame, we sometimes need our partners to remind us of life-giving truth.

After I returned from the game and Lisa offered me empathy, giving me a deep sense of togetherness, she also pointed me to something powerful that could start to guide me out of the onslaught of shame.

"Steve," she said gently, "even as you feel all those things, know that your worth is not defined by wins and losses. What happened tonight doesn't determine who you are or how loved you are."

Her words comforted me and soothed me and quieted my shame script.

If you are the one being pursued while feeling shame, and your partner is showing you this kind of tenderness and care, you can dare to let them in. To allow them to see you as you are. To trust they will accept you in all your imperfections and stay near you.

We will have fear, and it will take courage to rewrite the script, to move away from, *If my spouse fully sees me, there is potential for judgment,* and instead think, *If my spouse fully sees me, we can overcome this shame in me.*

Remember, our spouses can remind us of what is true when we are sinking in shame's lies. To help us see that no, there is not something fundamentally flawed about us. And yes, we still have worth when we fail. Yes, we still have value when yesterday's traumas seem to diminish us. We cannot overcome shame in isolation. But we can with their help.

Rewrite the Script

Once we let our partners in, they can help us rewrite the shame scripts that have been leading us through life. But how can that happen if we don't know what our script is? How can we be found if we don't know where we are?

We can begin by examining our internal scripts, the foundation of our shame. What we believe, think, and feel about ourselves is always guiding how we relate to our spouses.

Ask, *When do I feel shame? What do I tend to say to myself when I feel shame?*

Maybe it is, *I'm not smart enough,* or, *I'm not athletic enough,* or, *I'm not attractive enough,* or, *My need is silly and dumb.*

Look for where your shame might be rooted: *How did my parent respond to me when I had a need? Was there any hint of judgment?*

Consider how you coped with shame. *When did I feel shame as a child, and how did I react?*

Usually the truest answers to these questions take much reflection and time, so be patient with yourself. Take all the time you need. And allow your partner to be part of your processing so, together, you can start rewriting your internal script using truth.

Create a Shame-Free Zone

As you explore your experiences of shame, hold on to the big thoughts from our discussion here.

- Feeling shame does not imply there is something wrong with us. It is a common feeling.
- We cannot overcome shame and develop resilience to it in isolation. It grows exponentially when we hide it. We need our spouses to help us endure, recover, and heal from the shame we feel.
- When we share with our spouses what we are feeling, shame loses its grip on us.
- If we can become aware that shame has a goal of disconnection, we can begin to develop new responses to a familiar feeling. There is no shame in feeling shame.

Let's close this chapter with a visual that can help set the tone for you and your partner moving forward.

Picture the prodigal son returning home, miserable with shame. He is absolutely dreading the coming judgment. Then, to his shock, his father doesn't berate or condemn him or even give him a cold shoulder. His father runs to him and embraces him (Luke 15:11–32).

Here is a beautiful and stunning response to shame, one that reflects the heart of the Father toward us.

This is what we need when we are consumed by shame. We need a pursuing love. An embrace or a gentle touch. An attuned response. A kind reminder that we are loved for who we are. We need to be found, accepted, and celebrated.

The prodigal son's father created a *shame-free zone* for his son. And our Father invites us to do the same in our marriages—to offer, create, and develop a *shame-free zone*, a place where we aim to lessen our partners' shame and draw them away from its grip. There, we rehearse together who we are.

Our name is not "ashamed," but "beloved."

We are not deficient, but delighted in.

We are not rejected, but honored.

A Note from Lisa

We long to be known. And yet we are terrified to be known.

Our terror is connected to shame, which keeps us locked in narratives of being unknown. Shame whispers, *If they really knew you— your failures, your family secrets, your true desires and needs—they would reject you.*

Our longing to be known and desired is often so deep and unmet that when we find the one who says, "I choose you," we throw caution to the wind and leap forward with hope. We head to the altar having only scratched the surface of being known.

After six years of dating in high school and college, Steve and I felt known and loved. Safety was at an all-time high. We felt ready for the bliss of married life, for more of the sweetness we'd tasted together. And as the bud of the oak tree that was our new marriage sprouted, we were oblivious to the massive roots that lay below the surface.

Over time, we reenacted our childhood stories and encountered the shame embedded in them. As old narratives appeared, we struggled through the aftermath of our long-unmet emotional needs.

In my family of origin, expressing emotional needs was equivalent to exposing inadequacies. For example, one day in third grade, I had a humiliating experience at school. When I came home feeling mortified and deeply upset, my mother became displeased and frustrated. She was irritated with my sadness, and I felt shame. I learned through numerous occasions like this one that it was unsafe to expose feelings like sadness or fear.

As my emotional needs became my enemy, I became profoundly disconnected from who I was and believed shame's lie: *I must not matter.* I found little comfort from my mother and tried to repress my emotional needs in order to survive.

When there is no comfort for us in our emotions, especially in sadness, our shame becomes deeply wounding. And when we develop strategies to mask and numb our feelings and desires, it is almost impossible to access those feelings and desires later in life without a sense of self-judgment.

For years, I was fully committed to the false narrative that I needed to be an unattainable version of myself in order to maintain Steve's love—similar to how I functioned with my family of origin. Shame told me, *Don't let anyone in.* Revealing my true self—with my vulnerabilities, flaws, and fears—would make me less desirable.

The shame script that most impacted our relationship was linked to my appearance and my longing to be attractive to Steve. I was convinced that I needed to be everything he would want in order to hold his gaze. Whenever there would be a disagreement or conflict between us, I'd fear that I'd lost his interest, and I'd panic. Shame would whisper, *Your fear is a pathetic response. Your lack of confidence is so unattractive. He'd never desire the real you.* I was often paralyzed by shame.

Instead of expressing my feelings of sadness or fear with Steve, I allowed these thoughts to fester in self-contempt. As I rehearsed my shame script, my self-judgment became more deeply embedded within me, and we became disconnected. Because I lacked attunement to these feelings as a child, it didn't occur to me that I could share these needs and desires with Steve.

Shame keeps us locked into patterns that sabotage the goodness of attunement and connection.

After years of fighting this battle of shame, Steve and I entered a season of therapy due to our inability to communicate about our sexual intimacy. We began the arduous journey of bringing our needs, fears, and vulnerability to each other in a contained environment. And we began to reestablish safety.

We became more attentive to the whispers of shame, both in ourselves and in each other. We were more aware of the shame in misattunement in our childhood narratives. We noticed how sensitive we both felt when we sensed misattunement from the other. And we began to see how much we struggled with bringing our needs and desires to each other for fear of rejection.

Ironically, this was precisely what had drawn us together in the early stages of our relationship! As teenagers, we'd both been starving for attunement, so feeling known and desired with each other felt euphoric.

It was clear that we needed to tend to our roots with kindness and care, and that is what we did.

We cultivated safety, which allowed us to see and know each other in new ways.

We unearthed hurt, need, and desire.

I expressed my feelings of inadequacy and my hesitancy to share feelings of sadness and fear with Steve. He was able to be curious and empathetic.

We could say, "What happened to you?" rather than, "What is wrong with you?" We brought each other a spirit of curiosity—it was invitational, with no judgment, accusations, or demands. As we shared our stories in the safe place we created, shame began to lose its grip, and our damaged roots began the healing process.

Offering empathetic curiosity and vulnerably sharing our fears, needs, and desires has unexpectedly caused our marriage to flourish. We feel known and loved for who we are. Shame's whisper has become less audible over time. I don't feel as bound to the narrative that I am unlovable or unwanted. When I respond to Steve with empathy, and he responds to me with empathy, shame doesn't have as much power as it once did. We have grown in experiencing authentic care and tenderness together, which reminds me that *I am chosen.*

eight

Laying Down Your Weapons

Dan

Do you show contempt for the riches of his kindness,
forbearance and patience, not realizing that God's
kindness is intended to lead you to repentance?

ROMANS 2:4

Y ou wouldn't believe how constant her negativity is. And her passiv-
ity . . . it's infuriating!"

An intensely angry, cold man was describing to me, in the presence
of his wife, how *she was the problem*.

Jon chronicled Janet's reticence to engage with him, her impervious
silence, and the cost of the tension in their marriage. As a highly visible
senior pastor, he wanted to keep the community's respect and project a
rosy picture of his family life.

Janet appeared unmoved by Jon's diagnosis of their marital conflict,
offering little to affirm or contradict his opinion.

"What's your perspective on all this, Janet?" I pressed. "And how do you hope this time in therapy will affect your marriage?"

She shrugged and said, "I honestly don't have much hope for anything different—other than Jon having someone else to talk to besides me."

Janet was coming across detached from the conversation, but I could tell she was watching me closely. I also sensed she was hurt and angry.

Before I tell you what I said next, know this: the beginning of marriage counseling is a high-stakes crapshoot, where I sometimes must take risks to invite honesty, establish trust, and set a direction for the coming sessions.

"Janet, you are married to a bully. He's likely well-meaning but still insensitive," I ventured. "And you know how to pull his chain while remaining on the edge of his chaotic reactions, without getting swept away in his rants."

There was no shock on her face. In fact, if Mona Lisa has rendered an inscrutable, mysterious smile for centuries, I got to see a quick facsimile. Janet's suggestion of a smirk hinted that she was far more involved than she wanted to indicate.

In a later session with these two, a misstep of Jon's surfaced, and he began heatedly justifying his actions. His initial explanation was brief, then he shifted into a series of complaints about Janet's tendencies to overreact and shut down. In the fifth minute of unending patter, he exhaled enough air to harrumph.

Janet side-eyed him, then looked down at her lap.

I intervened with an obvious question that had, sadly, never been posed to this man. "Jon, are you aware of what your wife might be feeling now, after your five-minute diatribe?"

He looked at me with disdain, as if I were asking him to do the ridiculous act of performing heart surgery with a butter knife. "No. I don't generally put a stopwatch to my thoughts as you seem to have done."

The room reeked with contempt. Janet's face was filled with scorn, though moderately veiled. Jon's disdain for my probing was fuming out of him.

Contempt changes the energy in a room like cranking up the volume of a heavy metal song. This is true whether it is direct, like Jon's, or indirect, like Janet's. We find ourselves feeling contempt in the midst of conflict; we feel pulled into it by a fierce current. While not every argument has to lead to contempt, it is the instinctive experience.

The more intense our conflict, the more hurt we will likely feel—and the more contempt will become part of our relational dynamic. In the face of contempt, we unwittingly pull out the weapons we have used to protect ourselves, which only leads to greater division and even less safety. We felt driven to pull out weapons during past exchanges, and now our hands rest on our gun holsters as we do daily life.

A Danger We Can Accept or Reject

No marriage can thrive if contempt is a frequent theme. It is the number one killer of intimacy and hope, functioning like a deadly gas filling the air and poisoning the relationship. As we settle into patterns of resentment, we don't realize the danger we are tolerating.

Contempt is like a foul odor we are at first disturbed by but eventually acclimate to. Becky and I once lived downwind of a turkey farm, and in early spring when the wind changed, we thought we were going to die from the stench. After a few days, though, we grew accustomed to the foul odor. Our experience with contempt is the same. It may be pronounced early on in our marriages, leaving us agitated, but over time, we adapt and ignore.

Here is the good news (although I admit it won't sound too grand at first): *Contempt has power to the degree it is ignored and denied.*

If we pretend it is not there, or stubbornly step around it, it will inevitably lead to greater division and distance, even divorce. But once we begin to name it and explore it, contempt loses its poison.

Where Contempt Comes From

Tracing the origin of contempt brings us back to familiar territory: *shame.*

Contempt is to shame as smoke is to fire. Smoke can be blinding and toxic, and it is nearly impossible for it to dissipate until the fire is put out. First, we feel shame; then, we move into contempt, hurling judgment at our partners or ourselves—which lifts us, temporarily, above the abyss of shame.

Both self-contempt and other-centered contempt work this way, although there are distinctions between them. Contempt is made up of the same DNA irrespective of its direction. To understand it, we must return to the experience of shame.

Shame causes a fragmentation of the self. If fear sends us into flight, and anger activates fight, shame seizes us; we are wholly consumed with the desire to disappear. As young children, we covered our eyes to gain a sense of vanishing. As adults, we turn our faces downward to disengage; we cannot look up to see what we presume will be disdain and rejection.

How do we save ourselves from this moment of trapped misery, this soul disintegration? We find salvation in killing desire—the component that makes us vulnerable.

Desire involves uncertainty and risk; we are hoping for something we've not yet gained. If I want a burger and Becky doesn't, it is no big deal to me because my desire for a hamburger is not deeply attached to my soul. If, on a special weekend away, I want to make love and she seems bored, I feel something different than not getting a meal I want. My desire for a sexual moment is bound to struggles in our marriage, past abuse, and my identity as an attractive person.

When my soul-connected desire is dismissed or seems desecrated, I feel shame—more shame than I can bear. I decide that my desire must die if I am to live. *Contempt enables me to kill desire in myself and make desire dangerous for my partner.* Embracing it allows me to go on both the defensive and offensive while conveniently covering up my vulnerability.

How Contempt Works

One of Becky's and my earliest fights that escalated to World War III happened prior to our wedding during a conversation about a pewter tea service tray we were given. The tray symbolized for Becky a warm and inviting home where she could serve others delicious drinks and scrumptious food. She talked about how she looked forward to slowly buying high-quality furniture to give our nest a welcoming presence.

This immediately irritated me. "We won't have room for a tray that big in our car—it's a monstrosity! And our apartment is ridiculously small. Where would we put that thing?" My language was laden with hyperbole and belittlement.

She pushed back, sounding defensive. "You know the tray will easily slip in with little problem. Why are you against owning something nice?"

I upped the ante. "You may have forgotten I am not so princely paid as an assistant pastor in a church. Our financial future may not be able to accommodate you and your tray. Plus, do you not see how people will think we're putting on airs with our little tray?" Shame was fueling me. I could not bear that I would never be able to provide for the daughter of (what I perceived to be) a rich stockbroker's family.

Becky paused. "We will be able to afford nice things over time," she responded softly. "We don't need anything quickly, and, if we save, I'd rather get a few good pieces of furniture than Kresge furniture."

The word *Kresge*, calling up visions of K-Mart, triggered me, and my demeaning contempt sprang into rage.

I roared, "Well, if you can't live with cheap furniture, then I should forget the pastorate!"

I then slammed my fist on the dashboard and, in the furious cold of one of Ohio's most frigid winters, the dashboard shattered.

The violence of the moment hung in the air.

Becky turned away from me. Then I drove her back to her parents' home, infuriated, ashamed, self-justifying, self-contemptuous, confused, and feeling alone.

The war had begun over the disparity of our desires. She wanted beautiful things for our home. I wanted to be a good provider. I actually didn't care about the issue of having a pewter tray; I was terrified of being seen as incapable of earning enough to please Becky. Shame is always at war with desire.

And, again, how do we cope? We ditch our desire and turn to contempt. Though it is destructive, it momentarily anesthetizes and protects the fragile self, and takes vengeance on the one who exposed our desire.

The Two Directions of Contempt

In most marriages, one partner is more expert at self-contempt or at other-centered contempt. But none of us have only one form of it, because self-contempt and other-centered contempt are interrelated; if one is present, the other is not far.[1]

Whether we're turning inward or outward, our shame is in reactive mode, and it is flinging the weapon of contempt. Let's get a better sense of what each direction looks like.

Turning Inward

Self-contempt, as a concept, can be a little mind-boggling. If we already feel shame in the presence of another, why would we add to our shame by shaming ourselves? And how are we even able to do it?

Self-contempt is *the shaming of the part of ourselves* that we judge to be at fault for our shame. This does not involve a multiple personality disorder; this is how all of us work.

For an illustration, we can consider my ongoing struggle with misplacing my car keys.

I am often chaotic and inconsistent in returning my keys to the designated and agreed-upon location where they live. If I toss them in a corner for a second before I do something else, I quickly forget I've done it. Later, when I look for my keys where they are meant to be, I get flustered and angry. The words that rise inwardly are, *You idiot. What in the hell is wrong with you? Why can't you do something as simple as put your keys where they belong?* Notice how the question is not a true query but an interrogative that is nothing but a judgment.

Why would I shame myself with such a heap of contempt? The answer has to do with the fact that we are multiple selves. We have many parts that interact with each other in our interior. We have young parts that hold roles or experiences of our childhoods. We have older parts that take on tasks and roles related to our marriages, children, work, church, and hobbies. Are you precisely the same person at your son's soccer game as you are in a religious setting? Of course not. And it isn't just because of context, though that is an important dimension. It is truly because we are accessing different parts of ourselves in what is expected in each setting.

There is likely an angry and tough part of you that blames the weaker and more helpless parts of you for the suffering you have endured. The smarter part takes vengeance on the part that has felt stupid and incompetent for a long time. When we chastise and attack the part of us that is to blame, a part of us feels powerful and back in control.

Turning Outward

It is easier to understand the function of other-centered contempt. It attempts to blind the one who is exposing us. You shame me, and, whether it is intentional or not, I'll shame you. I know you judge me, and I am enraged. Our defensiveness, self-justification, and need to explain are fueled by other-centered contempt.

I was running late getting home one day, and my phone was dead, so I couldn't let Becky know. When I finally arrived, Becky was angry, and—before I even heard her out—I gave a biting explanation. It was delivered with the energy of defense and subtly implied that she was being insensitive, stupid, and inattentive to my plight. She in turn got defensive at my defensiveness, adding contempt to contempt, and we were off to the races.

Sometimes the whole exchange begins with a simple raised eyebrow or a passing smirk from our partners. Instead of turning inward and reviewing the long litany of our failures and flaws that would warrant such treatment, we clap back. "What's going on with you?" we might ask. It is our tone, not necessarily our words, that marks the terrain as contemptuous. We're going tit for tat here. Usually the escalation grows, and each increment demands a more heightened degree of offense and blame.

How We Use Contempt

We already have seen a number of expressions of contempt, but let's get a good grasp on three main ways we use it: numbing ourselves, protecting ourselves, and issuing vengeance.

To Numb Ourselves

Contempt can be used as a temporary fix in our agony of shame.

My clients Dalisay and Andres provide a picture of this. Dalisay saw herself as a princess after being pedestaled by key people in her life, including her mother's boss, who made Dalisay his pet project to perfect. She came to believe that if she were to own any personal flaw, she might cost her mother her job and prime future. Dalisay was considered a prize—on the condition that she fulfilled the dreams of her family.

As a result, Dalisay was desperate to avoid being exposed as having flaws (self-contempt for her imperfections) and was also frustrated with her mother's ambition and pressures (other-centered contempt).

Dalisay's contempt spilled out on Andres. On occasion, she would erupt at him, which made her feel powerful and above any complaint he might make about her. Throwing her contempt at Andres relieved her fear of being exposed, which, for her, was like a release of dopamine, a temporary escape from her agony.

Andres, on the other hand, was genuinely beloved by his parents, and he loved them too. The weight of his world came from his desire to bring them joy and from knowing success in school and a career would please them. He did well in school, but he had zero interest in the respectable career path they hoped he'd choose.

Whenever this came up in conversation, Andres remained silent, refusing to tell them about his passion for designing computer games. It would appear frivolous and demeaning to his parents, who'd achieved the impossible dream of rising from poverty to high standing in their impressive fields. Andres's desire to create innovative and compelling video games felt like an illegitimate one. The very thing that most moved him and gave him life was fused with a sense of shame. Andres went on privately loving computers and programming and spending his free time in the secrecy of his true love. It is not hard to imagine how self-contempt grew in that dank soil.

When Dalisay would raise her voice at Andres and demand a response, he found it easiest to comply and follow her lead—and he hated himself for doing it. As he felt the pangs of self-contempt and internalized Dalisay's scorn and contemptuous demands, he would cope by retreating into the gaming world. Self-contempt worked for him like a dissociative blanket he could crawl into whenever he felt her coldness.

Whether contempt turns inward (as self-criticism or self-blame, regularly assuming problems are your fault) or it turns outward (regularly finding fault with others, blaming others for one's own failures, and taking a stance of being more competent and in control than others), the same dynamic is at play. It is minimizing the inner hemorrhage of shame. It is like rushing to an injured soldier on a battlefield and frantically sealing their gaping wound to momentarily stop the bleeding.

To Protect Ourselves

If you think bullets might be flying toward you, what do you do? You put something in front of you to shield you—and, ideally, to bounce the bullets back to your attacker.

This is a maneuver of other-centered contempt we use to avoid facing our own culpability. The best defense is a good offense, after all. We make an accusation of our partners and rest safely in a sense of our self-righteousness. We accept the consequences of triggering shame in our partners and severing the bond of love between us.

It can be harder to see how self-contempt is protective, but it goes something like this: *If I blame myself before you have a chance to find fault, I have an antidote to your poison. I have already drunk the poison and not perished—so what can your vitriol accomplish?* It is subtle and counterintuitive, but it is a shield that impales in order to keep your sword from doing any more harm.

Most of us have become so accustomed to the protection of contempt that it now feels like our clothing, our essential outer layer we cannot do without. So we do not give up contempt easily, even when we are aware it is killing the marriage. To function without it, or even less of it, is to brazenly walk into the potential of being hurt buck naked. Revealing our naked desire—which could be dismissed, dangled, or desecrated—is too much to bear without the shield of contempt.

To Issue Vengeance

Finally, we use contempt to exact revenge. One of the hardest truths to admit is that we want our spouses to pay. For most of us, it is not a preplanned, anticipated, joyful delivery of evil to wound the other. Instead, we are reacting. We defend and attack in a split second. The response of immediate contempt is grooved deep into our cells and requires almost nothing to activate. It is a reflex of the soul. This doesn't, however, justify or explain why we want someone we love to suffer.

It is nearly impossible to address these issues without first reckoning with our self-righteousness—not in the sense of our moral character, but in our operating systems. We are desperately and unwittingly committed to whatever has worked for us to survive.

And the reactive pattern has even blended with our sense of identity. It is not merely my method of defense or attack; *it is me*. It is my personality, and it has always been me, and either you need to accept me as I am or let me be and leave.

These are massive self-justifications and explanations wrapped up in a porcupine suit with quills ready to fire. And if you get a quill, you deserve it—because no one should expect me to change. I am entitled to stay as I am. I will hurl a judgment at my partner that is meant to wound and feel justified doing so.

Vengeance is a refusal to wait for the slow work of repair to restore the injustice that has been suffered. In taking the execution of vengeance into our own hands, we simply repeat the harm that was done to us by escalating the hurt to a new level. The other player will call our hand and raise the ante, which only brings more harm to our hurt.

No More Turning on Each Other

As contempt pervades the air of our relationships—as shame eats at us and we react by wielding weapons—we will increasingly disconnect from each other. Conflict will become more frequent, or we will simply remain in a defensive position while carefully never addressing what divided us.

Let's pause for a moment and accept our humanity. The goal of this discussion is not for us to experience more shame for feeling toxic emotions, for hurting, for wrestling, for failing. It is meant to help us face reality and handle our pain in new ways.

Humans will always struggle with the disparity of desire and with shame. But *the way* we struggle, and the degree to which we invite humility, care, dignity, and intimacy into it—that is up to us. And there is a massive difference between our instinctive, cruel, highly damaging reactions and the honest, compassionate, togetherness-building patterns available to us.

Let your thoughts go this direction: *The next time I feel shame and contempt, I don't have to get trapped there. I don't have to address my tender, hurt places on my own. My partner and I can invite God's compassion and love into my deepest wounds.*

All this is possible. We move into healthier, unifying patterns by learning to reckon with shame—to catch it as soon as we see signs of it, relentlessly explore it, and grow closer to our partners in the process. We might be able to spot the smoke of contempt before the fire of shame, so it can be helpful to try to address contempt first.

We must come with real openness and a willingness to look at it. Many people I've worked with fail to see their own contempt—even though, as we've said, *contempt has power to the degree it is ignored and denied.* It loses its poison once we begin to name it and we refuse to move into any other discussion until it is explored. This is how we save ourselves from shame. We can never change what we fail to name, so we must name what is felt as true.

But what if naming our contempt only incites more shame and contempt? Following this impulse causes people to go years, even all their lives, without addressing it; they're convinced it will simply make matters worse.

I will not lie to you; it may, at first, do exactly that. But transformation is a process, so you must be patient. Addressing contempt means opening a door to what must be dealt with, and you may find a series of hard things to work through.

Admittedly, the temptation after opening the door will be to turn around and ignore it all. But if you see a wild batch of weeds, do you just pretend they're not there because of the effort required to pull them? Do you let them take over the land and crowd out all the potential good

LAYING DOWN YOUR WEAPONS

fruit? No, not if you love that land. You put on your gloves and bring your energy and focus to the task, keeping the larger goal in mind.

You will feel scared. And it will be hard. But you can feel those things while moving toward the life-giving path of kindness, grace-giving, and deep connection. You can resolve to keep your eyes set on it with your partner, saying, "We know we will struggle with these realities all our married life, but we vow to each other that we want ours to become a contempt-free marriage." That powerful intention alone can begin to disrupt the power of shame and contempt.

So start building awareness of what needs to be addressed. Keep in mind that we always identify the log of contempt in our own eyes first before we attempt to address the speck in our partners' eyes. Go back through this chapter asking questions like these:

- What aspects of contempt feel most familiar to me?
- How do I seem to use contempt to numb myself? Protect myself? Make my partner pay, or make myself pay because of my own flaws or failures?
- What DMZs do we have in place?
- How might contempt from my past be playing out in the present?
- What shame might be connected to my contempt?

As you do, invite into your heart attitude the change agent of defiance: Refuse to let hurt, anger, or past failure determine the future of what you can create together. Establish a stance of "hell, no" to death in all its forms.

Shame and contempt are toxic and deadly, so we must meet them with what is even more potent: the love and life of God. There is nothing he cannot defeat. Keep opening yourself to him so he can overpower them through you.

A Note from Becky

Volatility and contempt were the daily food and drink of my family of origin. My parents constantly judged, criticized, and mocked my siblings and me—and nearly everyone outside of our family. I came to assume this was normal and learned to adapt, finding ways to keep the "normal" from drowning me.

This upbringing readied me to respond to a husband who's prone to heating up and speaking with robust intensity. I'm quick to broaden my stance and dig in my heels. I've had lots of practice taking slow, controlled breaths with a heart pounding fearfully hard.

While Dan's contempt is overt and hard, mine is usually sneakier. I tend to hide my fury, and when the intensity becomes too scary, I want to shut down and go far away so no one can reach me. Other times it seeps out passive-aggressively.

A few years into our marriage, Dan and I were at a restaurant with friends, having a great time, when Dan mentioned something significant to the group he'd not previously shared with me. I felt unseen and hurt. In retaliation, I said something inappropriate and unkind about Dan. This was a pattern that played out on numerous occasions.

I feel such shame writing this now. Forty years later, I can see how I was following the model of my mother's piercing tongue. How many times had I watched her feel hurt by my father, then slice and dice him mercilessly?

As someone who typically loves getting along and hates conflict, seeing my own contempt disrupts my sense of identity. Normally I'd rather eat self-contempt than serve other-centered contempt. I don't want to think about how I can make someone pay when I feel hurt or ashamed, and I don't want to even address self-contempt. If it weren't for Dan's insistence that we address his failures of love, I'd gladly cruise through our blow-ups as if they were bad storms that "just happened" and left a bit of debris to clean up.

Take, for example, our fight about the pewter tea service tray. I never did acquiesce and say, "Dan, being with you is what matters most. Cheap furniture *would* be enough for me, given our passionate love for each other."

I didn't see our socioeconomic differences as a big deal—and I didn't explore his sense of a financial threat. I saw it as needless and stupid and didn't look closer.

In fact, when Dan's anger exploded and he pounded on the dashboard, *I felt delight.* I breathed calmly with the self-righteous satisfaction that he looked ridiculous while I looked immaculate.

I now can describe my struggle with contempt as a trauma-bound protective layer against more shame.

When I was in high school, the cultural belief was that a woman could gain power only through attaching herself to a man, and my mother enthusiastically ascribed to this. She put unrelenting pressure on me to date—with the ultimate agenda of marrying well—and viciously ridiculed me whenever I was not asked to a dance or other event. In a myriad of ways, the message was clear: *You must get married, and to get married, you must learn how to entertain a date.*

As dating became a focus, I was awkward and judgmental toward my own physical beauty. I also, somehow, felt excited and self-righteously confident that I could elicit a boy's interest. More than anything, though, I was fueled by a resolute commitment never to face the disdain of my mother or again sense from her: *You are not desirable enough to get a date.*

When I went out with boys, I seldom let my mother know where we were going. She'd wait up for me to return from dates and check that I didn't stay in a car with a boy. What would the neighbors think? I knew her strict standards and made sure that I only kissed boys out of her sight. My defense was to stay out of her way and—to the extent that I could—defy her quietly, only pretending to do what she wanted.

This was how I survived, and it created a behavioral pattern of contempt.

This intersection of sneakiness, anger, and shutting down, of course, has not served me well in marriage. Doing this with Dan has only perpetuated harm. It is not who I want to be.

Dan and I have found that it is crucial to name the presence of contempt. This is not at all easy, and we fail often. But more and more, when one of us feels contempt—whether from the other or within ourselves—we acknowledge it. This invites us to *get below* the contempt to what is driving it, which is always some form of shame.

I recently did a live Zoom event with Lisa, offering information about the marriage retreats that she, Steve, Dan, and I all lead together. Dan listened in, and as we got coffee together afterward, he asked, "How did you feel about your time?"

I grimaced slightly. "I think I did a C-minus job."

Dan gave a small smile and was quiet for a moment. Then he gently nudged, "Did you want some self-contempt with that mocha?"

While I felt exposed, I knew he was not letting me get stuck in self-judgment.

It was awkward, I thought. *And I wished I had been clearer.*

"I thought you did well—really well," Dan said.

I struggled to let go of my judgment and hold on to his words.

But then I reminded myself: *Dan has been honest with me about my weaknesses, so I know I can trust him when he delights in my strengths.*

Having a deep-rooted marriage means not letting contempt grow into a thick weed that keeps plants from growing in good soil. It requires a joint vow to not let contempt in any form take precedence over love. It requires stopping conversations, as Dan did, and not letting judgments pass as if they are no big deal.

Addressing contempt helps us clear out the weeds and gives us room to plant what we most want to cultivate: love.

nine

Leaving No Room for Feeling "Left"

Steve

Love is stronger than fear, life stronger than death,
hope stronger than despair. We have to trust that
the risk of loving is always worth taking.

HENRI NOUWEN

You boys want to go down to the park with me this morning?" my father asked, leaving my brother and me blinking in surprise. It was a highly unusual occurrence for him to invite us to do anything with him besides weeding flower beds, and even that was sporadic. With intrigue and disbelief, we jumped into the car with him.

But as my brother and I sat with my father on a green patinaed park bench, it became clear that we weren't there simply to enjoy fresh air and quality time together. We'd been summoned to a "big talk," which began with this shocking pronouncement: "Your mother and I have decided to separate, and the three of us are moving to Leavenworth, Kansas."

I remember these words now as if I heard them yesterday, not decades ago, and they completely shattered my reality. *What?! How could this happen?* I knew my parents sometimes didn't get along, but I didn't think much of it. I certainly never imagined living without one of them.

My father was being stationed in a new city for his job, and my mother was refusing to go with him. They were choosing to break apart the family, even divide us across the country.

Not long after that, my father packed a U-Haul with our belongings, trailered his yellow MG sports car behind it, and started driving us from Virginia to Kansas—what would become my seventh home in my eleven years. As I rode and looked out the window, I was still so stunned and confused.

How could it be possible that my mother had decided not to live with us? She was okay with not seeing us every day? We weren't important enough to her for her to find a way around this, to not allow *a thousand miles* to separate us—really? Didn't she love us? I was losing access to the only primary caregiver I'd ever known, and I was having trouble imagining a life without her. How could it be that she wouldn't be making a sandwich for my school lunch or telling me good night at the close of each day? What would I do when I needed a hug from her or wanted to see her after school?

I had a multitude of questions and nowhere to take them. There had been no further dialogue about my parents' separation. No direct engagement from them whatsoever. I had to grapple with the terror of abandonment privately and find a way to cope with the pain of being deemed "not worth being with."

From that time onward, I learned to protect myself from experiencing this kind of pain again by never getting "too" close to others. It became, in fact, a lifelong protective response. For decades I only leaned into relationships where there was little risk of the other leaving. I allowed a select few access to my internal world. How could I trust others? I'd been gutted by my mother choosing to leave me. I couldn't bear that kind of wounding again.

The reality of abandonment rings true for many of us. At some point along the way, someone we trusted abandoned us in a physical or emotional way, and in response to it, we formed a core belief: *I don't matter.*

We then either succumbed to this view of ourselves, feeling miserable and stuck in it, or we strove to reverse it and make ourselves matter. We hoped to prove—to ourselves, to others—that we were worth being with by achieving and gaining attention and favor. We turned to performance to establish our value, desperately wanting to believe, *I'm worth being chosen.*

Humans are born with a core fear of abandonment. We are terrified of being left. It is our baseline, and when it becomes part of our story, the fear intensifies.

Abandonment can take a number of forms; you don't have to have a story like mine to experience it. Maybe you, like countless others, felt emotional abandonment not through a singular event but through repeated, ongoing occurrences of feeling ignored and unseen. Perhaps someone important to you offered only a cold, harsh presence that communicated that meeting your emotional needs was off-limits. Many of us look back on our stories and find that, in some way or another, at times we felt overlooked, dismissed, or left emotionally or physically, and we couldn't understand why someone didn't engage with us or respond to us in our distress and need.

And we were wounded by this.

Emotional Neglect

Let's think back to the Still Face Experiment we discussed in chapter 5, when a young girl loses access to her mother. The mother is physically present but doesn't engage, and this triggers a sense of abandonment in the child. The girl screeches and points, frantically trying to get the mother to engage. In various forms of *protest*, she exerts emotional and physical energy to evoke a response. When a trusted person will not engage or respond, they signal to the other the *threat* of abandonment.

When infants are born, they use sounds and actions to communicate their needs to a parent—whether it's hunger, pain, discomfort, or the desire to be soothed—all with the hope that the parent will respond. These many cues and clues prompt the parent to engage. And what happens when a parent does not respond? The child finds herself living in a *still-face home*—a space with no emotional engagement.

Years ago, I worked in therapy with a young boy, Johnny, who was struggling academically and socially. He ate little and rarely slept. He was clearly distressed.

The way he described his home dynamic is still a vivid memory for me. His father would come home from work, sit in front of the TV, and drink a few beers. Johnny would eagerly try to engage his father: he'd talk to him, he'd ask him to do things with him, he'd run circles around his father's chair, through the kitchen, and back through the living room. All the while, his father ignored his son. Johnny constantly found himself asking the agonizing question, "Why won't my father respond to me or play with me?"

It is a classic picture of emotional neglect, a form of abandonment. Johnny felt disoriented and was unable to regulate his confusion and profound loneliness. Sadly, a parent can be physically present but emotionally absent.

Another client, Sophia, also grew up in a still-face home, with a mother who was cold and distant and rarely engaged with her emotionally. If Sophia revealed any emotion, such as sadness or disappointment, her mother sent her to her room and told her not to come out until she was "all done being sad." Her mother was unable to be a soothing presence to Sophia when she needed comfort.

When Sophia was ten, she was passionate about performing and she auditioned for the lead role in a school play. Her mother had reluctantly signed the school waiver, allowing her to participate. When Sophia found out she didn't get the part, she was devastated. She came home in tears. Her mother said nothing. No curiosity. No emotional engagement.

This was just one of many moments like this for Sophia. She ultimately felt like an orphan in her own home.

The Past Is in the Present

These are just a couple examples of how abandonment can look, but yours may be different. Perhaps in some other way you seemed to be overlooked or dismissed, you felt alone in your distress, or you were hurt as your needs went unseen and unmet.

However it looks for each of us, we, unsurprisingly, have brought that wound of not feeling valued or prioritized by someone in the past into our marriages. In everyday moments, we are quick to perceive that we are not a priority to our partners. Abandonment left us wary of intimate relationships, finding them extremely risky, particularly the one with whom we said, "I do." We know all too well that, at any point, our partners could suddenly leave and not return. We live with the imprint of the message past abandonment gave us—that something else is potentially more important than us and our connection may not be secure—and it informs how we react in the present.

This certainly has been true for me in my relationship with Lisa.

It surfaced once when Lisa spent a long weekend away with friends, enjoying some time of play—walks on the beach, thrift-store shopping, delicious meals, delightful conversation. I encourage Lisa to get quality time away with her friends like this, and we usually stay in touch through a text or call every day we are apart. On this trip, however, I didn't hear from her at all.

On the third day of no communication, I was agitated and anxious. *Is something wrong?* I kept wondering. *Why isn't she calling me?* I became preoccupied with my growing irritation.

My feelings were not connected to ego-based possessiveness but to the distress of my concern about whether Lisa was okay and my fear of being forgotten, being left, being "not worth staying for"—just like my eleven-year-old self. A past version of me was interacting with my present moment; I again felt the pangs of lost access to my mother while sitting in a U-Haul. While I consciously knew that I was far from my past, my subconscious returned to the old wound without my choosing it.

When Lisa returned, I felt upset, insecure, and unsafe in our connection, and I hated that I was bothered at all. I couldn't bring myself to engage with her. I was sitting on the couch reading when I heard her car pull in the driveway, and I immediately ran over to the kitchen sink to start washing some already-clean dishes. When she walked in, she came over to me and tried to hug me, but I was having none of it. I kept my back to her as if she wasn't there.

This, of course, was by no means a healthy, ideal response (it pains me to even admit I did this); it was a default coping mechanism related to my past wounding.

My experience of feeling abandoned by Lisa—momentary as it was—had triggered familiar feelings of shame: *I'm not a priority. I'm not valued enough to be remembered. Something else is more important than me.* My knee-jerk reaction was to ignore her; I was desperate to hide from my pain and fear of more abandonment. I didn't want to acknowledge my angst tied to not hearing from her—that, as I'd lost access to her (and perceived her being okay with it), I'd felt thoroughly unimportant to her.

What felt harmless and truly meaningless to Lisa translated as a threat of abandonment to me. And my instinct was to pull away and self-protect.

The Imprint of Loneliness

Past abandonment pain can play out in the present in various ways. Sophia (who grew up in a still-face home) and her husband, Jake, sought therapy due to the intense loneliness Sophia was experiencing in their marriage.

When Jake and Sophia would be in a conversation, and Sophia would begin to share how she felt sad or disappointed, Jake "went away"—he'd shut down and withdraw. He'd be unsure of what to say or do, so he'd say and do nothing.

When Jake wouldn't respond to Sophia emotionally, she experienced familiar feelings from her upbringing. Distress, fear, panic. Her body remembered moments with her mother. Whenever she'd needed reassurance and comfort, *her mother had turned away.* And now when she needed reassurance and comfort from her husband, *he also turned away.*

Her mother's emotional neglect left Sophia in a lifelong battle with a profound sense of isolation, which carried into her marriage. As we discussed in chapter 3, chronic loneliness often reflects unaddressed trauma, and many of us experience this.

In 2023, the US Surgeon General released an advisory declaring loneliness a public health epidemic, deeming it as dangerous as smoking fifteen cigarettes daily.[1] Unbelievable, isn't it? Research reveals that loneliness increases the risk of heart disease and is associated with higher rates of depression and anxiety. Clearly we are not meant for this; we are meant to be seen, known, and connected.

Loneliness is different from occasionally feeling lonely; it is feeling *alone*, fundamentally separate. We are hardwired for human connection— true connection. If we're in the presence of others, but if we don't have any sense of connection, we still can experience loneliness.

Emotional Presence

Maybe you struggle with loneliness, like Sophia did with Jake. Or maybe you feel the threat and pain of abandonment when your partner seems distant, like I did with Lisa.

When our bodies feel a familiar old pain, our default response will be to live out the past in the present, to do what we've always done to self-protect. But, instead, we can learn how to consciously disrupt the pattern and create a new story in the present.

We often need to help each other do this.

Sophia shared her past story with Jake and opened up about her present-day feelings and needs. It felt like a risk, but that's what set things in motion. As Jake became more aware of how his wife had endured such heartache and despair from her mother's emotional neglect, he began to respond differently to her. He gained insight about where she was coming from and the kind of emotional presence she needed. A new *awareness* of how Sophia's past story was being remembered and experienced in the present became the turning point.

As Jake saw how his lack of emotional engagement was reenacting his wife's previous despair with her mother, he slowly began to engage emotionally. He actively listened and asked questions. His empathy grew. He offered words of comfort and reassurance. He brought an emotional presence to his wife that reminded her that expressing her emotional needs to him would invite him to move toward her, not away from her.

Over time, the intensity of Sophia's loneliness began to lift. Healing began to occur.

Emotional presence is incredibly powerful because our desire for presence is innate. It is in our nature to long deeply for someone to see us.

The other day I was pushing my four-year-old grandson on a swing. I glanced at my phone, and within two seconds, he roared, "Watch me, Papa!" For a moment, I had "left"—and he'd noticed. The presence of another tells us that we are seen. We are not forgotten. We matter. We are chosen.

Many of us have come into marriage with a story in which presence, curiosity, and reflection were missing or, at best, inconsistent. Pause for a moment and reflect on your experiences of presence. Was a parent or other adult present with you, not distracted? Emotionally engaged, not distant? Try to recall how that happened, what they said and did, and what you felt.

At the age of sixteen, I felt utterly alone in my life, and that's when I found Jesus. Or, better said, he found me. I began meeting with Bill, a youth leader at the church I started attending. We sat in a dingy, greasy pizza parlor for a couple of hours every other week. He asked me questions over pepperoni pizza and endless glasses of root beer. He was curious. He was kind. He was present. I had never experienced this type of attention, focus, and emotional engagement before. Bill was a consistent presence in my life for a few years, providing something critical that had been missing: emotional presence.

"We are born looking for someone who is looking for us," therapist Curt Thompson wrote.[2] The internal question we ask of our spouses is, *Am I chosen?* And being chosen is revealed through presence and access: *Do I have access to my spouse's heart? Access to their story? Do they have curiosity about my heart? About my story?*

And our partners are asking the same of us. They are impacted when we look at our phones more than their eyes when we're in a room together. When we don't offer emotional presence by paying attention to their words, facial expressions, and indicators of what they're feeling. When we don't look closer with interest.

Curiosity and Validation

Curiosity is foundational to emotional intimacy. It says, *I want to see you. I want to know you. I want to be with you.* Curiosity reminds us that our partners chose us—and are still choosing us.

Curiosity is an intentional engagement with our spouses. It can sound like, "I was thinking about you today during your board meeting. How did it go for you?"

"What was it like when your friend stopped by to see you today?"

"Sounds like it was a difficult conversation with our daughter. Want to talk about it?"

Curiosity reminds us that we matter. It offers a sense of presence to our spouses.

Combining the change agents of curiosity (a desire to know and understand what the other feels) and kindness (a fierce commitment to enter the heartache and fear of the other with compassion and care) results in a powerful catalyst for reengaging and reconnecting after conflict.

When I was triggered from not being in touch with Lisa while she was away, and I reacted by hiding and withdrawing from her, her response was to offer a sense of presence. Even when I pushed her away, she came closer.

"What is it? What's bothering you?"

I remained silent.

"Steve? I'm here."

Pause.

"I love you," she continued, "and I'd love to know what you're feeling right now—whatever it is."

She was coming to me with emotional presence, curiosity, and kindness. Her behavior said, *I want to see you. I want to know you. I want to be with you.* She created a safe space for me to step into, to come out of hiding and be honest about my fear.

I started to open up and look at my experience with her.

I won't claim it was a perfectly smooth road from there. She got defensive (she wanted to be fully present with her friends, time slipped away from her). I got more agitated (whatever the case, the message I received was I didn't matter to her). But the process of reengaging had begun, and we were gaining each other's point of view.

The turning point for us came a little later, when we sat down for dinner. Lisa offered me kindness, saying, "I get that you were bothered, Steve. Of course you were."

That was what I needed. The complexity of repair was found in the simplicity of validation. When validation is offered, we feel soothed. We feel regulated. We feel understood.

She also said, "You always, always matter to me. A break in communication doesn't mean I don't want to be close with you. My love for you isn't going anywhere."

Her reassurance spoke directly to my old wounds. In that moment, she was adding a little brick to the path of healing I was on, helping me move forward with her into a new narrative we were writing together.

We all have some kind of wounding, and we all will be triggered at times. It's not that these moments ought not to occur; what matters is how we respond to them.

Will we be aware of our default reactions and be honest about them with our partners? Are we willing to reengage and reconnect, even when our bodies remember a familiar pain?

Also, will we choose to look closer with curiosity when our partners are triggered? Offer them emotional presence, listen, and validate their struggle? Imagine a new way to move forward together?

In these marriage moments we have the opportunity for a redemptive experience. With our partners, we can disrupt the old patterns and create a new story in the present.

Jumping from the Merry-Go-Round

Steve

*You can't go back and change the beginning, but you
can start where you are and change the ending.*

C. S. LEWIS

Justin and Whitney both work full time and have four kids at home. It's an exhausting stage of life. Justin's work often causes him to come home later than expected, and Whitney is drained by the time he arrives. One evening, Whitney saw Justin take a phone call in the car before walking into their home and was outraged. As soon as he stepped in the house, she unloaded on him.

"What are you thinking? You know I'm in here by myself with the kids!" she fumed. "Why is work always more important than me? I shouldn't have to take a number to get your attention—I'm your wife!"

Justin reacted defensively. "It was only ten extra minutes. What's the big deal?" Then he quickly deflated. "I just can't do anything right. I'm never good enough," he huffed, resigned.

As the oldest of five children, Whitney often had been tasked with caring for her siblings while her parents socialized. Her body was remembering something familiar: resenting being the responsible daughter, despising feeling alone, and raging at her parents for being absent.

Justin also was remembering a familiar feeling: receiving rigid demands from his harsh parents, failing to meet their standards of perfection, and hearing their contemptuous judgments about how he couldn't measure up. He'd find himself throwing up his hands in exasperation. "They're never satisfied!"

Both their bodies felt a past pain in a present moment, and they reacted. It was the kind of interaction they'd had with each other over and over.

Another client, Camille, grew up with a volatile, violent father, and although she diligently avoided getting in trouble, she could not always escape his wrath. There was no rhyme or reason why he would hit her or yell at her. She coped by leaving the house whenever she sensed he might be upset, running away from the threat of harm.

Camille went on to bring the same instincts into her marriage. One day her husband, Ryan, came home early and heatedly continued a tense conversation they'd had that morning. She responded the way she usually did when Ryan was upset: she took a guarded and defensive posture, then abruptly left the room. Camille fled to protect herself, just as she'd learned to do years before.

Humans are association-making beings, tending to make pairings with events. Camille had paired anger with harm. While she "knew" Ryan wasn't her father, her brain functions of cognition and reason were hard to access amid a threat (as we discussed in chapter 6). When fear kicks in, she just reacts. *And she keeps doing it.*

We all do a version of this. Today we inhabit the same bodies that experienced fear, hurt, and shame in our early years; they *know* where we have been every day of our lives. While we may not spend time consciously thinking about our past painful experiences, our bodies remember them, no matter how long ago those experiences occurred. And when the body feels it all over again, it reacts, sometimes in surprising ways. *And we keep doing it.*

We're instinctively seeking safety to protect ourselves, just as we did when we were younger. Our bodily reactions are natural and necessary, and they give cues about the ways we need care and what deeper hurts need tending to. But we can slip into those reactions repeatedly without thinking, causing us to pull away from our spouses in the process.

The two couples above—Whitney and Josh, Camille and Ryan— were in the rut of reenactment, doing what they'd done countless times, before and during their marriages. They were reenacting past traumas and survival strategies, *and* reenacting a particular marital conflict on a loop. At this point they knew their lines well and could predict how each would respond, not to mention how their connections would fracture. They needed to learn how to stop themselves from becoming slaves to their automatic reactions and prevent further division in their marriages.

Dan and I repeatedly see couples caught in reenactment, and we experience it in our own marriages. It's a familiar pattern for most of us—a merry-go-round that won't slow down, leaving us stuck on it as it keeps spinning. Until we learn how to jump from it.

Survival Strategies That Hurt Each Other

To move toward disrupting this cycle, let's look closer at what it is we're doing, beginning with the harm we're bringing to the present and the hurtful dynamic we're creating.

We experience something that triggers a felt experience of a past trauma. Then we naturally reenact behaviors that have, in the past, enabled us to survive heartache—but these are not productive in the present. Instead, they lead to defensiveness, accusation, and division. We could even say that these self-protective rituals bring psychological sabotage into our partner dynamic.

Dan and I have seen this kind of harm a thousand times in marriage counseling. One partner feels so hurt and angry that they blurt out severe judgments and vicious accusations. Even if the words reflect some reality, they are not spoken for the sake of the truth or for any hope of reconciliation. The person is simply exploding their frustration and contempt in desperation to find relief.

I was hurt, and I will hurt you in response. I will make you pay for the harm done unto me. This is how reenactments are justified and reinforced.

The reenactment of feeling triggered and slipping into survival strategies happens nearly as fast as the speed of sound. Once the process begins, it is like stumbling. You can know you are beginning to fall and wish you could self-correct, but gravity takes hold, and it is impossible to extract yourself. Usually, the best you can do is minimize the impact of the fall. Tragically, few of us know how to fall well without getting hurt or ramming into someone else.

Removing the Cloud of Judgment

Triggers themselves are not the problem. They simply expose a deeper issue: hurt-generated patterns that have long been used to escape the vulnerability of *shame*. We often cope with shame by flinging judgment at our partners, then use that judgment to justify our behavior.

Let's look at a few ways this could play out in a partner dynamic, considering each person's perspective of the same experience.

Jocelyn: He rarely gives me a chance to finish my thoughts before he pounces.

Diego: Whenever she tries to tell me how she feels, it's like she's wandering around aimlessly in a house of mirrors and dragging me with her.

Joel: She is so quick to assume I'm not telling the truth that
I become anxious and preoccupied with ensuring every
detail can be backed up with proof.
Anika: He never fully tells the truth. It seems like he's
constantly walking on eggshells and then, out of nowhere,
blames me for being judgmental.

Clara: He wants to make love but never really asks, only hints.
And he does it when something else is happening, which
makes it hard for me to say yes.
Luis: She is so scheduled and precise that I feel like sex has
to be written on the calendar a month in advance, or the
answer will be no.

Each couple is telling some truth in their reflection of a marriage
conflict, yet taking little to no ownership of their part in the tension.

Judgment is contempt that condemns without considering context
and disguises our part in the problem. Judgment against our partners
and ourselves is like a cloud preventing us from being able to see what's
happening.

I must emphasize that judgment is a way we cope with pain. It temporarily protects us and relieves us from the hurt we feel—and yet it
reinforces the reenactment cycle.

What if we could take judgment out of the equation? It takes a tremendous amount of courage to do this amid tension, but let's imagine it
for a moment and see how much more room for curiosity and honesty
we'd have. Consider those scenarios we looked at above with judgment
removed.

Jocelyn: I wonder what keeps me from saying things more
directly and what causes him to feel out of control when I
don't.

Diego: I do feel something tighten in my chest when she can't seem to say what she wants to say, and that must increase her anxiety.

Joel: The truth has always been hard for me to address since I grew up constantly feeling under the microscope of my dad's scrutiny. I suppose that could be connected to my tendency to gather proof to validate myself.

Anika: I hate that he feels so much fear when we talk about conflicts. I know I have some of the same tendencies to question him, just like his father did.

Clara: It is hard for me to admit, but I resent his sexual overtures. They come across as cowardly to me, maybe because my sexual desire has always seemed to be stronger than his.

Luis: It's easier for me to think she is too particular about when we have sex and quick to push me away. But it's far more challenging to admit that my past sexual abuse and struggle with pornography have left me feeling bad about sex, and I want her to take that feeling away.

Removing the cloud of judgment enables us to see more of what's really going on. But gaining this type of awareness is only the first step toward change.

Disrupting the Familiar Patterns

Knowing at a logical, executive-functioning level that our self-protective behaviors lead to more harm, unfortunately, does not mean we'll stop doing them. Even if we "just try harder" to avoid doing them, we'll only build momentum for an even greater crash at a later point.

Our goal cannot be to fully remove reenactments, triggers, and shame from our lives, because that simply is not doable. We will continue to wrestle with these thorns just as we wrestle with sin for the rest of our lives.

Our triggers are so deeply embedded in our brains and bodies that to erase the source would be to erase the mind. And while shame is a trauma, it also alerts us to matters that are at the core of who we are and who we are meant to become. Besides, having no shame would mean we also would lack empathy and conscience.

So what *is* the goal? To become quicker to engage the trigger and understand clearer how to disrupt the process of reenactment so we can open ourselves to healthier responses, healing, and connection.

To do this, we need to identify what our bodies remember and engage with our trauma stories, which takes great courage. The more we can enter our own stories of harm with kindness, the more attuned we can be to our spouses' shame cycles. And the more the process is a shared privilege and calling, the more likely it is that kindness will repeatedly interrupt the cycle and leave us open to the work of healing.

We will spend the rest of this chapter exploring what this can look like.

Welcoming a Wake-Up

We often aren't aware that our bodies are remembering something familiar; our bodies just react. We may not even have words for what we feel. We need to awaken to the past hurt we are remembering in the present, to what is causing us to reenact what is familiar.

Sometimes we need help to do that, which was the case for Mike.

Mike and his wife, Lori, enjoyed guiding their two young kids through their nighttime routine, but by the time they'd given good night kisses and turned out the lights, they'd be exhausted. While Mike would want some relaxing together time, Lori would be ready to collapse into bed.

On one evening this played out, Lori started to walk upstairs to go turn in, and Mike became agitated. Surprising himself, he suddenly erupted, "Why are you always going to bed so early?"

This became a merry-go-round of conflict they got stuck on. Mike would regularly become irritated and upset in the evenings, sometimes coping by having more than a few drinks and then giving his wife the silent treatment the next day.

As I sat with Mike and Lori, he asked, "What's wrong with me? Why am I having such a hard time with my wife going to bed earlier than me?"

"It could be that your body is remembering something hurtful," I replied. "Sometimes the body reacts in the present based on something from the past. So, if you're willing, let's think back to what pain you could be pairing with these present moments."

Mike shared that when he was sixteen, his parents decided he needed to move out of the house and live with his aunt and uncle because of significant conflict between him and his parents. He felt incredibly hurt, rejected, and abandoned.

And now, as his wife would walk up the stairs with her back to him, he again had a sense of losing access.

"I wonder if there is anything familiar about your wife leaving you and walking up the stairs," I said to Mike.

Mike paused for a moment, then answered, "I'm not sure."

"Perhaps it's connected to something in your story," I suggested. "Particularly when you lost access to your parents."

Mike started to tear up and slowly nodded. It was a tender moment, and Lori gently moved closer to him.

Sometimes past traumas lie dormant, leaving us unaware of their impact or even how we're feeling them in the present. Mike was willing to be curious about his experience, about why he was feeling and reacting the way he was. And his humility made room for me to help him see what he couldn't see on his own.

Pushing others away might be easy, but receiving loving help is brave.

One choice perpetuates harm, the other invites healing. Sometimes we truly need to allow others to look at behaviors with us and help us be intentional about remembering the past pains we are carrying.

Feeling Safety and Reassurance

As we enter into intentional remembering, we need to create safety and receive reassurance that we can find comfort and kindness, not just more heartache.

On a trip to the Oregon coast, Lisa and I were walking on the beach with our golden retriever, Otis, when another large dog approached us. Otis normally greets other dogs with exuberant friendliness, so I was surprised to see him respond with caution. He pulled back with his tail up and the hair on his back raised. Instead of running to the other dog, he stood perfectly still and watched him. I wasn't sure what about the other dog's posture or look could have prompted this, but I could tell Otis felt unsafe, even threatened.

At one point Otis turned his face to me, looking for reassurance. He took a few steps toward the other dog, then returned to nudge my leg, again seeking security. It was as if he was asking, *Am I safe? Am I okay?*

I patted him on his head and bent down to ruffle the fur on his back. "It's okay," I told him kindly, finally figuring that something about this other dog was reminding him of his past hurts. Looking at his uneasy face, I thought, *I get it, pal.*

Humans are far more complex than dogs, of course, but this gives us a glimpse of how we are wired to respond to possible threats and what we need in those hard moments. We are designed with deep survival instincts; we look for clues that we're safe, and if we don't sense them, we will seek them out (whether through self-protective, divisive behaviors or through emotional support from our spouses). We legitimately need a sense of comfort and protection.

"It's okay," I said again to Otis. "Go ahead."

Soon he relaxed and slowly ventured toward the other dog, and within a few minutes, they were chasing each other up and down the beach. That small reassurance from me helped him move toward what he feared and play with a new friend.

We all need this, whether it's in a moment of fear, feeling past harm, or simply feeling disconnected. We crave comfort and kind words in a tender tone, a reminder that we're safe in our spouses' presence.

This touches back on what we discussed in chapter 6—how we need to create safety when we sense a threat, how we need to pause and direct ourselves away from getting swept up in the stress biochemically crashing on the shore of our brains. Let's think of some ways we can do that for our partners and for ourselves amid reenactment.

Receiving Attunement and Care from Your Spouse

Through our therapeutic work, Camille and Ryan became in tune with how her body was remembering experiences with her violent father, especially when Ryan would react abruptly or unpredictably. Over time, Ryan developed a kind response to moments when her body remembered past harm. He recognized how his harsh responses were triggering Camille and worked to avoid prompting trauma responses in her.

He began to offer words of reassurance:

"I get that my abruptness startled you."

"I can see how that impacted you."

"I'll try not to react so harshly."

As Lori and Mike became more aware of how his agitation was connected to the abandonment he had experienced, Lori became more tender, compassionate, and intentional. Before walking up the stairs, she would make statements like:

"I get this can be hard for you."

"I'm not leaving you."

"I'll see you in bed in a few minutes."

Words of reassurance are a powerful antidote to painful memories.

Awareness is what helps us have a caring response. *Awareness invites understanding, and understanding invites tenderness.* After all, the body is remembering for a purpose; it needs protection and care. It is bringing attention to what requires care and advocating for deep needs to be met.

The goal is to create an atmosphere where we are quick to offer or receive this kind of awareness and tender care at a moment's notice—because our bodies can react in unexpected, even benign moments.

The other day Lisa and I were at a restaurant, and as she was reading a menu description to me, I got distracted and asked the waiter for some waters.

She lashed out, "I was talking to you!"

I snapped back defensively, feeling scolded.

In truth, Lisa's indignant response to my distraction was tied to past pain with her emotionally unavailable mother.

I was close to justifying my behavior, telling her she was overreacting, and minimizing her hurt. I was tempted to enter into reenactment, to step on the familiar merry-go-round.

But I paused.

And then it hit me: Lisa's body was remembering something familiar.

"Lisa, I'm sorry," I said softly. "I shouldn't have done that. Help me understand what happened for you."

She expressed more of what she was feeling, and I saw how distressed she was.

Whenever we see our spouses dysregulated like this, we can offer relational soothing:

"I realize my distraction was hurtful."

"I want to listen to what you are saying."

"What you are feeling is important to me."

We all will continue to have these kinds of moments in our marriages, no matter how much healing we experience, but we can learn to approach them and move through them in more patient and loving ways.

Receiving Attunement and Care from Yourself

We can offer this same compassionate curiosity and care to ourselves. When we feel disoriented or confused about why we feel the way we do, we can begin to attune to what our bodies are attempting to communicate.

The other day I was on the phone with Lisa, sharing exciting news about my pickleball tournament that had just finished. One of our daughters called, and Lisa said, "Oh, I need to answer this call from Ellie. I'll call you back."

As irritation crept in, the merry-go-round began to spin.

But then I paused. And I got curious.

I asked myself, *Okay, what's up? What happened?*

I was able to recognize that my irritation and frustration were connected to something familiar: the feeling of being a bother and inconvenience to my mother. I took a couple of deep breaths, allowed myself to be still, and offered myself a kind and tender response. *Of course you were bothered. You were hoping to connect with Lisa about the big game.*

Our bodies crave reassurance in distress, and when we don't have access to our spouses' reassurance, we can receive a kind, tender, soothing response from ourselves.

What's happening? we can ask ourselves. *Does something seem familiar? What might be familiar?*

As we remember, we also can offer words of reassurance to ourselves.

Of course that was overwhelming to you.

Of course that stung.

Of course you have a panicked feeling.

We can name these feelings and offer ourselves validation and comfort.

Remember when we said earlier that removing judgment can help us see more of what is really going on? This is true not only toward our partners but also toward ourselves. When we observe ourselves without any judgment, we can respond and tend to ourselves better. We find true answers when we say, *I wonder what would be helpful,* or, *I wonder what my body needs.*

The practice of attunement to our own bodies develops muscle memory. This not only gives us access to what we need but also equips us to disrupt reenactments with our spouses. We are quicker to explore,

How do I habitually protect and defend myself?

What are the explanations and justifications I repeatedly come back to?

What past harm might my body be remembering in moments of conflict with my spouse?

When my body remembers something familiar, how do I use judgment to perpetuate the cycle?

It's in these moments that we need to remember how powerful the change agents of humility and honesty are.

In humility, we are attuned and aware of what is happening in ourselves and our spouses and aim to disrupt the triggering of trauma, past and present.

In honesty, we uncover our own hurts and failures, and own what is ours without blaming our spouses.

As you resolve to embrace these transformative mindsets, linger with these words from theologian Barbara Brown Taylor: "To become fully human . . . means growing gentler toward human weakness. It means practicing forgiveness of my and everyone else's hourly failures to live up to divine standards. . . . It means living so that 'I'm only human' does not become an excuse for anything. It means receiving the human condition as blessing and not curse, in all its achingly frail and redemptive reality."[1]

Look for moments today when you can practice more of this gentleness toward frailty, grace toward failure, and openness to change.

Part Three

Generating Goodness Between
You and Beyond You

eleven

Reconnecting, Repairing, Restoring

Steve

The meeting of two personalities is like the contact of two chemical substances: if there is any reaction, both are transformed.

CARL JUNG

W here were some of the worst places you've been in conflict with your spouse? A family reunion? A big work event? A vacation? For Lisa and me, it was at a marriage conference—that we were leading.

In the early hours of the morning, we heatedly argued in our hotel room, and at one point I, predictably, left the room. I was frustrated and irritated and wanted to be alone. I walked out of the hotel with our bags and headed to the car, even though it was pouring rain.

As I was closing the trunk and getting completely drenched, I realized I had a choice to make. I could avoid going back to the room; I could return but be emotionally withdrawn; or I could attempt to repair things with Lisa.

This is the bind for each of us when conflict has driven a wedge between us and our spouses.

I began walking back to the hotel room and let my heart begin to soften, knowing I wanted closeness with Lisa more than perpetual disconnection. Even so, I felt cautious. A bit anxious. *Will this go well? Is it worth the risk?*

As I stopped in the lobby for coffee, I thought, *It might be worth it.*

I took a deep breath, made it back to our room, and approached Lisa with a soft expression.

"Can we try again?"

Conflict is inevitable in marriage. We will never be fully attentive and attuned to each other. We'll forget to pick up prescriptions and offer uninvited thoughts about where to park. We'll misread each other and forget what we agreed to. Our desires will be far from aligning. Whether they are related to mistakes or individual differences, everyday disappointments are part of our lives together and can cause division.

What also is inevitable are relational *ruptures*—failures that cause significant wounds and emotional distance. These failures might be words that demean or threaten the other, or choices made with no consideration of what the other will suffer. They could be any betrayal of the other through a pursuit of money, power, sex, addictions, or other false gods. We are flawed humans who fail. And those failures break trust and leave a wide emotional gap we cannot easily resolve.

Few of us instinctively know how to work through these divisive experiences. In this chapter we'll look at how to manage not only everyday conflicts but also relational ruptures, learning ways to reconnect, repair, and restore.

Conflict as Connection

First, let's look at how to engage everyday disappointments or frustrations, whether it is when a partner is running late, wants more social interaction than we do, or spends more money than we expected on a gift for a friend. The divide is not severe, but we feel tension as triggers and past issues keep us from seeing the other's viewpoints and joining them in good care.

A question I've frequently asked couples is, "What is the goal of your conflict?" After giving me a confused stare, one might playfully reply, "To win!" and the other might say, "To come to a compromise," or, "To resolve it."

These are logical answers many of us would give. But research tells us that if our only aim is to resolve our conflict, we'll be fighting a losing battle. Marriage expert John Gottman has found that nearly 70 percent of conflict is unresolvable.[1]

Yes—we spend a vast amount of emotional energy attempting to solve what we cannot. While this may seem like a defeating reality, it's actually a clarifying one: our work in marriage is not simply to resolve conflict but to integrate fruitful ways to stay connected to each other throughout it.

Another piece of research supports this. Professor Ted Huston discovered through a thirteen-year study with 168 couples that failure in marriage is not the result of conflict but of a weak emotional connection.[2] A strong emotional connection, not the avoidance of conflict, is a significant predictor of contentment in marriage.

Could it be that small-scale conflict is not the foe we make it out to be?

When we are in conflict, we reveal what we think and feel. Conflict is, in a sense, a form of *intimacy*, a word that originates from the Latin *intimare*, "to make something known."[3] It is a time when we give our partners access to ourselves. Conflict allows us to be seen and known (which we innately desire) and to be heard and understood (which are foundational components of emotional intimacy).

What if we approached conflict in our marriages with a reimagined purpose of *cultivating emotional intimacy*?

Automatic Reactions to Conflict

If your knee-jerk reaction to this is resistance, you're not alone. Most of us have learned to avoid conflict at all costs and assume it only can go poorly. We see it as a threat, and, as we've said, our bodies have automatic reactions to threats.

Let's review the four primary trauma responses we discussed in chapter 6, since our bodies often respond the same ways in conflict. We do these things to temporarily relieve the hurt, frustration, or disappointment we feel in a charged moment.

- **Flight**: We escape through withdrawal or retreat, disengaging or physically walking away. We avoid further conflict by removing ourselves from it.
- **Fight**: As our adrenaline spikes, our muscles tense up, our bodies and faces tighten, and we may shift to aggressive behavior. We believe we'll gain control if we exert power.
- **Freeze**: Our bodies shut down and are unable to move. We feel detached, do nothing, and hope the conflict passes.
- **Fawn**: We seek "safety by merging with the wishes, needs, and demands of others."[4] We pacify the other, hoping that prioritizing their needs will diffuse the conflict.

We learned these responses in our early years, whether we were adopting them to cope or watching our parents model them.

I recall a familiar pattern from my childhood when my parents would argue about monthly bills. Their voices would escalate, and my father would quickly leave the room. Then he'd slam the front door, jump in his car, and speed away. As an adult, my frequent reaction to conflict is to withdraw physically or emotionally. My instincts often mirror what I saw modeled in my family of origin. This "imprint of conflict" can be deeply formed in us and become an unseen, unnamed loyalty that drives us.

Seeing your partner or yourself do the behaviors above might frustrate you. *Why can't she stay present? Why do I always get so angry?* Remember, though, how judgment can cloud your view of reality and keep you from seeing what needs care. These responses are the body's way of protecting itself from potential harm. The amygdala is automatically hijacking the situation, but it does not need to stay in charge.

If you can honor how the past is revealed in the present and be kind to the body's natural need to protect itself, you can begin to develop an awareness of what you both need to feel safe. We've discussed the importance of pausing in intense moments to create safety, gain clarity, and invite connection. Let's look at a few more practical ways to do this.

Repairing Everyday Conflict

A driving force behind our flight, fight, freeze, and fawn responses to conflict is our preoccupation with *being understood*. When our partners overlook, minimize, or dismiss our feelings or thoughts, we tend to work hard to get them to understand us. We might become louder and more expressive, saying,

"That's not what I said."

"That's not what I meant."

"You're not listening to me."

Our hurt from feeling misunderstood fuels the conflict. We have distress in our bodies because we feel disconnected (and we crave connection). We may end up feeling stuck in tense misalignment. *Being preoccupied with needing to be understood leads to further hurt and disconnection.*

Engage Difference and Seek to Understand

Saint Francis of Assisi once prayed, "Grant that I may not so much seek to be understood, as to understand."[5] What if our goal in conflict was to offer understanding and validation? How might that change the dynamics?

Conflict often begins when we encounter differences of opinion, need, or desire. Differences can feel threatening and cause guardedness and irritation. *If you would think like me, believe like me, or feel like me, all would be well.*

How do you typically respond to the differences between you and your partner? Do you notice any judgment or mockery? Is there room for kindness or delight? Is there *curiosity* around difference?

You both are unique individuals wired in distinct ways. You didn't partner with sameness; you partnered with difference. Your partner's differences probably attracted you to them. It is no surprise that you don't always think and behave the same way.

So, yes, you will feel frustrated when they spend too much money, forget to feed the pets, don't call their brother, stay up too late, or would rather watch a basketball game than a movie. But you can view moments of conflict as an opportunity to engage difference. The key is to be free of judgment.

Lisa loves to read in bed at night with the light on. If I try to read at bedtime, I fall asleep within thirty seconds. Sometimes I'll snap at her, "Why do you have to read before bed?" which is essentially saying, "Why can't you be more like me?" There is a tone of judgment, implying she is somehow fundamentally flawed.

When we have this type of impulse, the courageous questions to ask are, What drives my belief that my partner should be more like me? Am I willing to let go of whatever is blocking my ability to be kind to their difference?

Instead, I might ask Lisa, "What do you like about reading before bed?"

And you might explore, "I'm wondering why you might be hesitant to call your brother."

Any needed problem-solving can follow ("Would you be open to trying a smaller book light for bedtime reading?"). *But we start with understanding and respecting our partners' individuality.* We sustain connection as we engage differences with kindness.

We also "seek to understand" whenever we see our partners bristle. When Lisa and I were discussing ways to spend a free weekend, she made a remark that, to me, implied she'd rather be with others than with me. This, as I've shared, is an area of sensitivity for me. Plus, Lisa typically finds time with others more energizing than I do.

I grew silent and cold.

"What happened?" Lisa asked, and an argument ensued.

Before long Lisa said, "I'm not sure we're headed in a good direction. Can we pause for a second?"

I sighed and took a moment, then said calmly, "I was hoping to spend time with you this weekend."

She softened. "Oh, I want that too. I get that my need to be with others can imply I don't want to be with you. But know that time with you is important to me."

What helped change the trajectory? The choice to say, "Hang on, can we pause here?" Pausing is a form of honor and of protection. It disrupts our automatic responses. It invites curiosity, and curiosity moves us toward connection.

Invite Them into Your Experience

I recently was home alone recovering from dental surgery and found myself irritated that Lisa was out of the house—although I'd previously agreed to it. Apparently I was late in realizing how much I'd benefit from her presence.

That night, after feeling miserable on my own all day, I expressed my frustration to her. I'm not proud to tell you what I led with: "Did it not occur to you to stay home today?"

Naturally, Lisa was baffled, as she'd simply carried out the plans we'd made together.

I needed attunement, comfort, and reminders that I was not

alone—but I found it difficult to name that in a way that fostered closeness. Instead, I issued an accusation, a type of demand.

Should I have simply ignored my feelings and not shared them with Lisa? That would have steered us away from immediate conflict—but there would've been a cost of further division. Attempting to hide our pain always robs us of the possibility of more intimacy.

The issue, of course, was my approach; how we begin these conversations dictates how they will turn out. Demands or blaming tones push the other away, and the relational experience we're hoping for slips out of reach.

Instead, we can say something like,

"It was hard for me when . . ."

"I was feeling a bit frustrated when . . ."

"I felt hurt by . . ."

This invites our partners into our struggle and gives them the opportunity to respond to our needs. We're giving them access, encouraging them to move toward us rather than away. We're creating space for them to see and acknowledge—without defensiveness—the impact of their actions.

Validate Their Experience

When the roles are reversed, it's easy to hear our partners' hurt as blame and become defensive. But, as we just said, when one of us opens up about a struggle, we're giving the other access to our needs.

We can choose to hear a judgment that we have done something wrong.

Or we can hear an invitation to give comfort and care.

At the very least, we can validate our partners' experience, which doesn't require agreement. We can offer it even when we don't have the same feeling or perspective.

When Lisa and I got to the root of my struggle of being alone after dental surgery, she kindly offered validation by saying, "I get that it was hard for you when I was gone today. Of course you felt lonely."

Sometimes this type of twenty-second exchange saves us from having a twenty-minute debate. Validation may be all we need.

Other times, validation leads us away from hostility and toward safety and support, even if we have conflicting desires. Seeking to understand and validate our spouses' needs throughout conflict maintains our connection.

Express Sorrow

When our partners reveal their hurt, we can offer comfort and care by expressing sorrow. Sometimes it's a matter of simply showing compassion; other times we need to admit a wrongdoing.

Humility, genuineness, and specificity are key. We only bring more harm when we trot out a generic apology that subtly blames the other for being too sensitive:

"I'm sorry you thought I was unkind."

"I'm sorry you were disappointed in what I did."

"I'm sorry you're unhappy because you didn't get what you wanted."

In contrast, when I have raised my voice at Lisa, repair has included my saying, "I'm sorry for raising my voice. That was unkind and wrong. Forgive me."

Repairing Rupture

Conflict can create momentary emotional distance, but typically, in due time, we can come back together stronger and more connected. This is not the case, however, when there is a rupture, which begins with some degree of betrayal. It might involve manipulation, condescension, addiction, abuse, deception, gaslighting, pornography, or affairs. Some type of mistreatment leads to deep distrust and forms a gap we cannot leap across by merely admitting wrong and asking for forgiveness. A rupture, then, is a divide that has not healed and has generated an infection.

Unaddressed ruptures can be ignored for a season, but they are like a serious infection: left untreated, it will tear down the immune system, spread to other parts of the body, and eventually cause death. As the divide continually deepens, the shell of a marriage may remain, but it will not have the capacity to grow, flourish, and experience delight.

Seeking to resolve deep rupture often begets even greater harm. I've seen some couples' attempts at repair cause more significant damage, which ultimately cost them their marriage. In the following section I'll suggest ways to avoid this, and in the guidebook Dan and I will offer even more specific guidance. It is crucial to have a plan and know how to move through it.

You also would benefit immensely from seeing a good marriage therapist, especially if you're feeling ongoing discouragement and disconnection. The deepest healing is possible when you have a wise and kind voice engaging with your stories and walking you through the process of restoration.

As we discuss the steps below, keep in mind this is a process, not an event.[6] It often becomes a long-term endeavor focused more on honoring the other than resolving the conflict.

Own Your Limited Perception and Propensity to Blame

We all are bent toward blaming each other, and our bias blinds us to key aspects of reality. Even when we have been wronged, we need to take whatever is blinding us out of our eyes first.

"In the same way you judge others, you will be judged," Jesus said. "Why do you look at the speck of sawdust in your brother's eye and pay no attention to the plank in your own eye? How can you say to your brother, 'Let me take the speck out of your eye,' when all the time there is a plank in your own eye?" (Matthew 7:2–5).

We might think, *I feel hurt; my partner obviously has harmed me. Why should I extract a plank from my eye when it's clear they have a sequoia in theirs?*

But notice: Jesus was not saying all sins are equal or that a victim holds the same responsibility as a perpetrator. He was exposing how blame sets us up to be blind. The issue is judgment.

After we're triggered, we naturally start blaming because it relieves some of our hurt, shame, and vulnerability, giving us some degree of power when we feel powerless. Blame, however, is a judgment built on *a biased reading of reality*. It fuels a self-protective defense and scapegoats the other while mostly taking ourselves off the hook. It keeps us from listening to each other and propels us into a rapid-fire tit for tat, upping the intensity of contempt.

Maybe the plank dominating our view is a desire to punish, a demand for immediate change, or an inclination to take responsibility for others' feelings. A plank is anything that keeps us from seeing reality. Removing that plank is not a denial or dismissal of the offense; it makes a healthier dialogue possible. Our hurt feelings remain. But we can choose to honor the hurt by not retreating from or attacking the other, but by staying present and honest so we can properly address and tend to it. The plank might be just the opposite, such as our inclination to take responsibility for what others feel. A plank is anything that keeps us from seeing reality rightly.

The goal is not to enter a dialogue with a spirit of opposition, determined to convince or silence our partners. The first move, instead, is to own our history, bias, and propensity to blame. We resolve, *I won't engage you or myself with contempt.* We set out on a journey of asking God for a true, nonjudgmental perception of ourselves and our partners.

It is through this contemptless, blameless engagement that we can begin to tell the truth.

Tell the Truth and Name the Harm

We are called to confess our sins to one another. The Greek word for *confession* means "saying the same thing"—essentially, not using words to avoid, muddle, or minimize the harm. We are to name reality as it is, not how we wish it were.

I've repeatedly heard one spouse say to the other, "But I didn't *intend* to do that": To be late again. To drink too much. To flirt with your friend. To take on another project. Posing behind *intent* is an effort to escape our darker motives and the impact of the harm we caused. I seldom hear a spouse name the hard reality that something was more important than their partner or that they (consciously or unconsciously) desired to make their partner pay. It's likely they were resistant to seeing it in themselves.

Telling the truth is not merely admitting what we are aware of; it's also opening our hearts to aspects of reality that are new to us. It's a posture of being willing to *discover* truth to the extent that we can say things like,

- "I'm late because I chose to take the work call and avoid a conflict with a client. I could've called him back tomorrow, but, instead, I prioritized him over you."
- "I said things at the dinner party that humiliated you—how you're chronically late, how you blame me for your tardiness. Their laughter made me feel vindicated. I was making you pay."
- "When you questioned me this morning, I put you off, offering only trite answers. Then I avoided you the rest of the day."

Notice there is no effort to defend, explain, or justify the failure. It's not contextualized by reminding the other of intent. It's the hard, heartbreaking truth. And the truth will set us free. Eventually.

Move from Contempt to Sorrow

As we look at the truth, contempt naturally will rise —and we'll need to release it before it does any more damage. This doesn't mean pretending the harm has disappeared; it means loosening our clenched fists and putting down our weapons of war. We're resolving, *The brawl of contempt stops now. I won't let this harm's impact spread any further than it already has.*

All harm produces shame and contempt, often toward ourselves for trusting again, or for failing again.

Releasing contempt after being wronged may sound like, *I will not let your harm determine how I give myself to you.*

Releasing contempt after failing may sound like, *I will not let my harm of you cause me to hide, and I will not blame you for my failure.*

Again, we're not excusing the harm; we're extracting the poison from the air so we can begin the hard work of grieving and honoring the loss. There can be no true repair without sorrow.

When we've failed, we'll feel so desperate to escape our shame that we'll promise the harm will never happen again. We'll buy gifts, take an exciting trip, and initiate make-up sex. But these all are shame stoppers, not true release. The shame remains. And we need to let it walk us to sorrow.

Under all shame is a reservoir of grief, generated by years of harm we've both endured and caused. We typically harden our hearts to it. But when we quiet the shame, we can begin to mourn specific failures and also long for all things—including our spouses, ourselves, and our marriages—to be "liberated from its bondage to decay and brought into the freedom and glory of the children of God" (Romans 8:21).

Releasing contempt is a radical act of defying human brokenness that gives us the comfort and courage we need to reengage a process of redemption. It enables our hearts to say,

I will not turn away.

I will not let death and decay have the final word.

I will let my mourning be the conduit to receive the comfort I need for myself and for you.

This process is not a one-and-done event but a repetitive choice to say "hell, no" to shame and "heaven, yes" to grief-fueled comfort.

The more we loosen our hands from the refusal to risk feeling hurt again, the more we'll receive what we need to address the consequences of harm.

Tend to the Consequences

Rupture is like a fragile bowl dropping to the floor and shattering. At this point in the process of repair, we gather the broken shards so we can start putting them back together. We hold each shard in our hands and examine where it fits. Practically, this means we look closely at the consequences of the harm and how they connect to our larger stories.

What was the impact of the harm?

How have our past trauma responses been activated in the present?

How did this failure repeat past failures in the marriage?

How are those memories connected to other losses and heartache from our upbringing?

Keep in mind we won't be able to hold the broken shards if we're still holding on to blame or shame. We can process the impact and learn from the losses only when our hearts are open and kind.

Kindness, as we have said, is a fierce commitment to offer goodness to ourselves and others. It is the choice not to rush the process, but to take time to understand how the harm occurred and where we find ourselves now. Sorting through the shards bonds us together in shared grief, gives us a clearer perspective of our stories, and sets us up for restoration.

Whether or not we're conscious of it, we all long to see beauty grow out of ashes. This is exactly what practicing repair ultimately produces. We experience restoration.

We learn to build trust and deepen intimacy. To expand the care we offer each other. To stand against the trauma our beloved has suffered and pursue healing.

We cannot, of course, stand against what we don't know. Restoration involves the slow unfolding of stories that give us access to what our partners have had to endure and tragically includes instances when we have replicated the harm of their past. Each time we engage one of these stories, we again move through repair: owning our bias, telling the truth, releasing contempt and grieving, and tending to the consequences of harm. In this sense, restoration is a process accomplished over a lifetime.

The Courage of an Open Heart

Perhaps you've heard of *kintsugi*, the centuries-old Japanese practice of repairing pottery using gold lacquer instead of clear glue. It highlights each piece's "unique history by emphasizing its fractures or breaks instead of hiding or disguising them. In fact, *kintsugi* often makes the repaired piece even more beautiful than the original, . . . giving it a second life."[7]

The method is based on a profound Japanese philosophy that brokenness can be tended to and made beautiful. It is the reversal of all that seems sensible. How can shards not only be brought back together but made stronger and more beautiful?

This depicts the mind-boggling claim of the resurrection—that death doesn't get the final word, all losses will be redeemed, and even the scars of the cross will reflect the glory of God.

This is the bigger story of restoration that our marriage stories get to reflect.

Repair in your marriage will defy logic and reasoning. It will feel both astounding and risky, especially as you give your partner access to hurts. But you are meant to be seen and known, to be honored and cared for, and you can choose to invite the deepest experiences of these things into your marriage. There always will be conflicts and ruptures for you to navigate, but as you grow stronger together over time, the duration of your disconnection will lessen and you'll find ways to cultivate intimacy amid tension.

Opening your heart to your partner is a courageous act that begins the process of mending what is broken. It shifts your loyalty from disconnection to connection and tells your spouse, *I choose you, and I choose us*.

See if you can approach your spouse not with the intent to blame, judge, demand, or harm. Instead, come with curiosity and softness, with kindness and safety, and with the defiant intent to bring them goodness despite both of your failures.

Explore whether your heart might say,

We both are imperfect and will fail. But we can choose connection and care with each other.

We both can heal and grow—there's more strength and beauty available to us. Let's stay close as we move toward it.

twelve

Walking Through Fire Together

Dan

Every atom of your flesh is as dear to me as my
own: in pain and sickness it would still be dear.

CHARLOTTE BRONTË

For years I did not like my father-in-law, Paul. I endured and limited visits with him. As our children aged, he loved taking them on motorcycle rides in his sidecar. I hated motorcycles and deemed them a scourge to humanity and a fool's errand. I tolerated his ancient BMW and Moto Guzzi, but I refused to ride on them.

Decades later, Becky and I moved to a small island about nine miles from Seattle that made transit to the mainland a nightmare in certain seasons—unless you had the privilege of being the first on and off the ferry as a motorcyclist.

I ate my past disdain and began to ride.

It was around that time that Becky told me, "If my father dies and you haven't made some attempt to get to know him and love him, I don't know how I will forgive you."

Her words exposed both my insolence and arrogance. I could be civil, if not polite, but I would not let that man have any of my heart.

Several months later, I set out to leave the house for an important meeting and couldn't start my motorcycle. Becky, feeling my panic and anger, offered, "I'll call my father and see if he can help."

I was so desperate I would have taken help from Beelzebub.

I soon found myself listening intently to Paul's voice through the phone as he graciously and wisely walked me through several issues that might have shut it down. The third try lit up the bike. I sincerely thanked him, and in one simple exchange, our relationship changed. Before long, I was inviting him to join a fishing trip to Montana with a group of good men and allowing him into my heart.

The stories about Paul that we've accrued over the years are wild, insane, and hilarious. His was a once-in-a-lifetime drama, equally upsetting and compelling. Over time, I came to love him—and not because he changed. I changed. It is now a horror to consider what might have occurred if Becky had not disrupted me and I had not needed his help with my motorcycle.

The story of my relationship with Paul displays truths that reveal some of God's purposes for love and can lead us to new levels of intimacy in marriage.

It is only love that enables us to understand and enter the beauty and brokenness of another.

It is only love that gives us access to the suffering of someone who has brought us heartache.

And it is only love that can transform heartache into honor and delight.

What grows the soul of a marriage is the practice of joining in the suffering of the other. We are not meant to be alone in our suffering. We are called to bear each other's pain and sorrow and, by doing so, strengthen and deepen the sinews of our love.

It is for this worthy reason that we will spend this chapter looking closely at how we can lament and ache together, specifically as we suffer each other's humanity, dreams, and death.

Suffering Each Other's Humanity

Over twenty years ago, scientists discovered in monkeys something they called *mirror neurons*. Further study revealed that these unique neurons also are present in humans and provide the neural foundation for empathy, giving us the capacity to sense others' emotions and mirror them.[1]

When someone smiles, we are apt to smile as well. When a newborn hears another baby crying, they orient their body toward the sound. We feel what others feel; we respond to their distress with our own distress.

Researchers also have found that entering the suffering of our spouses builds intimacy and marital satisfaction.[2] This correlates with the neuroscience truism that "what fires together, wires together."[3] *What deepens our emotional attunement increases our relational intimacy.*

And if we don't suffer for our spouses, we will not grow the roots of our love.

A number of obstacles, of course, stand in our way.

First, none of us are naturally inclined to choose suffering. We honestly feel unable to bear even our own suffering; how could we possibly take on more? We tend to avoid the shame that arises when hurt implies the other has failed. The flood sweeps us both away in the waters of hurt, shame, blame, and hopelessness.

Second, a tragic result of our trauma is that we've learned to shut down our emotional attunement to our own suffering, which also dulls our capacity to feel on behalf of others.

And third, consequently, we shy away from engaging with our spouses' human frailty and with our own. This leads us to offer less care than we could and limit the care we are willing to receive from our spouses.

Eight months into our marriage, Becky caught a stomach bug and spent hours vomiting. I held her hair back and made efforts to comfort her. She was astonished that I would stay with her when she was sick, even contagious; she couldn't recall anyone ever caring for her in such a state. But I'd vowed "to have and to hold" her "in sickness and in health."

When *I* get sick, however, I want to be left alone. It is not easy for me to feel awful physically and to bear Becky's presence and concern. In truth, I do not want my state of frailty to be on display.

Illness keeps us from functioning at our typical level of usefulness. We can't escape needing care, which can be an intolerable reality. Many of us with histories of significant trauma want to push through illness, avoid resting, and pretend like we don't need help. We resent care when it reminds us that we are frail.

But we are meant to suffer each other's frailty—and the stories that have turned our hearts against needing help. Looking at the past can inform the future, shaping the way we will handle friction and suffer together in the days to come.

If we want to write a new marriage story, this is a kind of new goodness, strength, and togetherness we don't want to miss.

One way to start changing our approach to struggling and hurting is to release some of our previous assumptions and, with curiosity, ask new questions.

- What if I don't feel that I can bear my own suffering because I am not meant to bear it alone?
- What if bringing my spouse into my suffering will enable me to step into theirs?
- And what if facing our frailty together brings us closer to God and gives us a clearer view of the bigger story we are part of with him?

Let's explore what moving in this direction can look like.

Groaning for Glory

Typically, when I say something to Becky about feeling hurt, wanting more from her, or suggesting there is a better way to go about a project, her first response is defensive. For decades, my reaction was to fight against her, and we'd be off to the races.

I understand her defensiveness vastly more today than I did even a year ago. I know to expect it when I disrupt her, and I now endeavor to respond with compassion and to enter *the groaning of God* on her behalf and mine.

It is a profound shift from my natural reaction to her, one built on the foundation of Romans 8.

There is a grand entrance and exit to this chapter in Scripture. It begins with the stupefying statement that "there is now no condemnation for those who are in Christ Jesus" (v. 1). Every fault, every failure, every form of darkness in our hearts melts before the presence of the one who is love.

The chapter ends with the proclamation that nothing can separate us from the love of God, whether it be death or life, angels or demons, or anything in creation (vv. 38–39). It speaks to our deepest fear of abandonment. We are not alone, nor will we ever be separated from God, even in our darkest failure, doubt, or anguish. We may abandon God, but the Trinity will never forsake us.

These grand promises hold the power to change our lives—but only if we engage with them. As silly as this metaphor is, these promises are like a gift card that sits in our sock drawer, pointless unless we draw from its potential. We have to participate in cashing in on the gift.

Romans 8:17 gives us a picture of what that entails: "If we are children, then we are heirs—heirs of God and co-heirs with Christ, *if indeed we share in his sufferings* in order that we may also share in his glory" (emphasis added).

We are called to enter the sufferings of Jesus. And we do so every time we enter the humiliation of Good Friday and the despair of Saturday on behalf of others.

Becky has known humiliation in the coldness of her mother, the violence of her father, the manipulation of boyfriends, the rape by a professor, and through my replication of several of her past emotional traumas. I enter the suffering of Jesus when I enter the stories of Becky's past.

Beyond suffering her past, I also suffer the future on her behalf, as I long for her to experience what is wholly good and beautiful.

This mirrors Romans 8:22–23: "We know that the whole creation has been groaning as in the pains of childbirth right up to the present time. Not only so, but we ourselves, who have the firstfruits of the Spirit, *groan inwardly as we wait eagerly for our adoption to sonship, the redemption of our bodies*" (emphasis added).

We are to groan with the earth, with each other, and with the Spirit as we await our complete adoption as God's sons and daughters. As intensely as a woman suffers in childbirth, we are to suffer for the earth and for each other, as the Spirit within us groans with words too deep to hear (v. 26).

Most days, I don't hear the groaning. I just live my life as if I am outside the keening. That is, until the Band-Aid of my distractions is ripped off, and I am face-to-face with death in any of its multifarious forms. Then, I groan. But I often fail to scan the horizon for redemption.

When I am suffering, I am not prone to wait, let alone wait eagerly. I want it changed now. *Right now.* And if not, then soon. *Very soon.* But I seldom have such eagerness when I suffer for another.

This is what we do naturally; it is not the "adopted by God" life available to us, as we read in Romans 8. That life involves the stunning promises of no condemnation or abandonment and the peculiar call to suffer with Jesus. To await eagerly our own adoption and our beloved's adoption. To suffer each other's long and arduous path for the redemption of our bodies.

What does that look like?

We can consider a simple example of everyday marital friction. During a visit at our daughter's house, Becky and I were disagreeing about when to leave. As she became defensive, I felt my anger rise. My habitual reaction would be to prioritize that anger and let it fly out at her.

But, in that moment, I made a concerted effort to let it go and, instead, tune into Becky's emotions and enter her suffering.

I imagined and felt the loss Becky would experience in missing a dear friend's birthday party if we left later.

I felt sorrow for her that most of her life she'd had to defend herself to survive.

More than anything, I felt a deep, almost inexplicable desire for her heart to one day be free from having to defend herself.

Groaning for her enabled me to change my plans and facilitate an early departure without feeling pressured or irritated.

This is, of course, an infinitesimally small example. If I had been more mature, this would not have been much of an issue.

Anytime I anticipate Becky's redemption, I am compelled to imagine my own, sparking desire for my own transformation.

When I am forced to face my younger, angry parts, will I groan for them to be redeemed, or will I threaten them with condemnation or abandonment?

Will I feel the eager, intense desire to become more of who I will one day be, or will I justify and defend my current irritation and remain stagnant in it?

These questions are our entry point for suffering our partners' past and future.

We also are called to suffer our partners' dreams for earthly tastes of the coming redemption.

Suffering Each Other's Dreams

Every dream is an anticipation of all that awaits us in eternity. Whether the dream is to fish the South Island of New Zealand one more time before I die or for my daughter to get the job she has spent months preparing for—all dreams are when we imagine goodness for ourselves and others. They are sweet sliver tastes of the banquet ahead.

The dilemma with dreams is that most die or fade in the cold, harsh reality of this world. Though the dreams of my thirties are entirely different from those of my seventies, the ones that crashed and burned left their impact on me. Failure lingers with us like scars on our bodies.

This is another way we are to enter into our spouses' suffering: to grieve their dreams that have died.

And what about dreams we have as a couple? They often involve individual pursuits and daily diligence, which can create obstacles to intimacy. Years ago, I wanted to get a PhD and then be part of starting a graduate school to train therapists and pastors in engaging story and trauma. Those dreams were not Becky's, but she understood and supported my passion, even as it cost us time, money, proximity to each other, and friendships.

There are costs to dreams, whether they end up fading or succeeding. We are meant to suffer the conception, gestation, labor, birth, and feeding of dreams together.

Most of us understand the suffering of a dashed dream. It is harder, however, to enter the suffering of success, especially when it has taken years and enormous labor to achieve it. Dreams that succeed can beget pressure and drudgery and turn into nightmares.

I have seen countless people exhaust themselves to earn a doctorate and then, upon reaching that goal, descend into depression and affairs. I have worked with a myriad of attorneys, physicians, and pastors who have slaved to gain the knowledge and credentials to practice in their field and now hate what they do. The despair of achieving what they thought they craved turned the dream into a mistress that inevitably betrayed them.

We are meant to suffer the dream, the cost to achieve it, the glory embedded in the desire, and the inevitability that no dream, whether successful or a failure, can provide what only eternity holds.

Sometimes our pursuits involve joining God in bringing light to darkness and carrying the burdens of his creation with him—and as we do that, we cannot avoid suffering the weight of it in our marriages.

Years ago, Becky grew close with women who had once been prostituted. Eventually, they invited Becky to join their Friday Night Outreach to teenaged, prostituted girls on the streets of Seattle. I would drive her to the ferry, bid her goodbye at 7:00 P.M., and return home to fret and pray. Sleep that night would be ragged. She'd be on the streets with the team until 3:00 A.M., then go sleep at our daughter's downtown condominium. When I'd pick her up Saturday morning, she'd be weary and traumatized.

After a few months, I noticed our tensions, especially sexually, were increasing. I sensed in her a burgeoning fury toward men, and I was the only specimen in the house. Arguments lasted longer and seemed to be fueled not by the topic, but from an underground reservoir of anger. Becky denied this, and, week after week, things spiraled.

Becky saw the violence and degradation that these girls were suffering every night with men who left their wives, drove to the city, violated a trafficked woman, and went home to their families. She could not bear the darkness and hypocrisy she was face-to-face with as the girls shared their stories with her.

Eventually, our marriage was saved by our weeping and praying together for the women she engaged. It didn't come quickly or easily but during our groaning together, the layer of rage, related to the many violations Becky has suffered with men, including me, came to be named and honored.

We are meant to suffer each other's failures and compulsions. We are to feel the weight of what our beloved suffers as they pursue the labor they are written by God to engage.

Suffering Death

We now turn to the most difficult discussion, a reality that I can barely allow to shadow my soul. The thought of living a single day without Becky is beyond the pale of what my body can hold. Yet, I must grapple with the possibility of not having my beloved by my side. So must you. If we don't, the unaddressed heartache will slowly sap our capacity to live well in the present.

To the degree we fear death, we will even more so fear life. If we refuse to engage with future realities, we also will resist engaging with our present moments.

If you are young, death feels like it is a morbid and distant threat. If you are in the so-called dying age, it is as near as your friend who passed most recently. But even when it is near, we often find ways to insulate ourselves from it. Our culture's approach to death is to outsource it. We don't die at home. We outsource death to hospitals and hospices. We wish to keep it as sanitized and distant as possible.

We do not want to wrestle with mortality any more than we must. We do not want to let ourselves feel the anguish of an earthly life ending or the reminder that we too will each one day take our final breath.

Yet it is as inevitable as waiting for the big trip to visit dear friends that takes a year to plan—the day comes. All the waiting is no longer in the equation as the door opens and those we love are there to welcome us.

If we can't sorrow now over our eventual departure, we will not be ready to do so when the day knocks. Our sorrow is meant to increase our wisdom. Psalm 90:10 plainly states that "the best of [our days] are but trouble and sorrow, for they quickly pass, and we fly away"—and this reality is not meant to increase fear or despair. It allows us to live with greater freedom and passion, alive to the present, anticipating the future.

The psalmist went on to pray, "Teach us to number our days, that we may gain a heart of wisdom" (Psalm 90:12). We must be taught to count our days. It is not something we will do without instruction. To number our days is to be aware that tomorrow is not inevitable simply because we have things to do and appointments on our calendars.

Do I really want to haggle over who did the dishes yesterday? Do I want to worry about paying off the credit card or going to my best friend's destination wedding? Is the conflict over what restaurant we eat at worth the energy, given this could be our last meal together?

Facing death helps us put things in perspective and frees us to view life as a gift, not an entitlement. If we live aware that our time is limited and our next breath could be our last, we can receive each day as a benediction, a word of blessing that could be a closing to our story. Every day becomes another, perhaps even final, chance on earth to taste and see that the Lord is good.

In my father-in-law's last hours of his life, Becky and her family surrounded him in his hospice room, and I flew in from a conference to join them. After nearly ten days of no food or water, Paul was so weak that he could only whisper.

At one point, he beckoned me to come to his side, and, as I put my ear close to his face, he asked, "How much longer will this go on?" I told him with tenderness that I knew he wanted to depart, and we honored his life and blessed him to go whenever he was ready.

A half hour later, Paul signaled for me to return. I saw a warmth in his dying face and a sparkle in his beautiful, Paul-Newman-blue eyes, revealing that he had grown fond of me. I again pressed my ear to his lips as he conjured enough breath to whisper what would be his final words to me.

"Eat more ice cream."

What? I'd clearly heard each word, and it made no more sense than if he had begun to recite the Gettysburg Address.

I looked him in the eyes and assured him, "I will, Paul. I promise." What I was promising at that moment was utterly obscure.

When I returned to Becky's side, she quietly asked, "What did he say?"

I repeated his words, and the look on her face indicated she thought I was lying or insane.

I have pondered Paul's last words to me many times since he passed. He knew that I worked too much and then played too hard to balance out the extremity of my life. And as a young boy, when his mother was dying of cancer and his father was absent, Paul had few pleasures other than ice cream.

I have come to understand his final words to me as a call to slow down, take in simple goodness, and enjoy what a bowl of ice cream can offer. I now can't eat ice cream without thinking of those last moments with Paul. His benediction offered an odd, disruptive blessing that both haunts me and makes me laugh.

It also brings to mind the words of the apostle Paul boldly mocking death: "Where, O death, is your victory?" (1 Corinthians 15:55). As much as death is a bully that traumatizes, it never gets the final word in our story. The final word is the resurrection and the promise that every dream will not only come true but also be infinitely greater than what we could imagine.

Meet the Good and the Bad with the Spirit

You are not meant to suffer alone, and neither is your spouse.

While we all are inclined to avoid our frailty and mortality, doing so will not change our nature. We are needy creatures designed to be dependent on one far mightier than us, and we live in a hurting world that is not yet redeemed.

Courageously facing hard realities such as these with your spouse will not only deepen your intimacy but also strengthen you, move you closer to God's heart, and make room for more joy.

It isn't a question of whether you'll suffer, but whether you'll suffer together and with the Spirit.

Will you live out *no condemnation* and *no abandonment* to your partner?

This is a way you can be the face of God to them.

Will your heart pang on their behalf for wrongs to be made right and for their complete wholeness, redemption, and freedom to come soon?

Maybe you'll groan with God for the *more* you know they're meant for and ache for the good and beautiful he is preparing.

Will you share the weight of your partner's dreams, knowing those pursuits are part of their unique wiring and calling?

If you do, you'll be entering the sufferings of Jesus.

It also isn't a question of whether you'll die, but how you'll spend the days you are given.

When was the last time you acknowledged that you and your spouse won't have countless days on earth?

Try echoing the psalmist's prayer, "Teach me to number my days" (Psalm 90:12).

Last, what would it mean for you to view life as a gift and as a chance to experience God's goodness on earth?

Perhaps you can give and receive benedictions that point to bigger truths than any current pain—blessings of love that mock death and reflect the promise that the resurrection gets the final word. That goodness wins.

As you and your partner choose to step fully into your sorrows together now, hold on to the fact that they will last only for the night, even if the night feels incredibly long.

Immense joy will come in the morning.

And it will last forever.

thirteen

Choosing Each Other Through Play

Steve

We don't stop playing because we grow old;
we grow old because we stop playing.

GEORGE BERNARD SHAW

W anna climb?" Lisa asked me, excitement dancing in her eyes.

We'd been walking along a beach when we came to a steep rock wall, and before I knew it, Lisa was scampering up the side of the mountain like a cat up a tree. She used to scale the trees in her backyard as a kid and has loved climbing ever since.

At first I gaped at her, amazed. Then I slowly followed her.

I was struck by how much delight there was in that moment and (even thirty-seven years into marriage!) found myself thinking, *Who is this woman?* She obviously felt free. Unbound and unleashed. I felt deeply attracted to her, utterly captivated, like when I first saw her at age sixteen and asked her to sign my yearbook.

181

I also noticed how connected I felt to her in this simple moment of play and how content I felt in her presence. Given the early parts of my story, when I so often felt like an inconvenience or a bother, Lisa's presence reminded me, *I am chosen.*

What Is Play?

All of humanity speaks the language of play; we were born with an inherent capacity and desire for it. One of our grandsons loves board games, particularly Trouble. When he plays it, there is joy on his face and delight in his movements. Nothing else matters; he is completely present. Watching him reminds me that all humans have an innate yearning for play and that, at every age, play is our most natural form of engagement.

This morning I played pickleball with some friends. We started early, and when I checked the clock, I was shocked to realize we'd been on the court for two hours. It'd felt like five minutes. The same kind of suspension of time happens when I fly-fish with Dan. We'll spend eight hours on the river together and it will feel like fifteen minutes. We all know this experience. As we let ourselves feel captured by play, we lose a sense of time.

Play is meant to cultivate delight. A child at a playground will call to their parent, *Watch!* The child longs for the parent to see and delight in them. We have that same longing in us as adults, and there is a purity to it. *Watch* communicates desire and invitation—both for our joy of being watched and for the joy of the other who watches us. It's what Lisa felt when I watched her scale the cliff and what I felt as I watched her.

As a faculty member at the Seattle School of Theology and Psychology, I taught a class on counseling children and adolescents for several years. Each semester, we'd spend our final session together playing a game of capture the flag along the shores of Puget Sound. As onlookers passed by, they'd give us curious looks. *What is this? What is happening?* It was a group of fifty adults playing with absolute delight.

182

When we are in seasons of difficulty, play often becomes less important to us. Over the years, as we experience more complexities of life—family, logistics, hardships, busy days—we can't even remember what it feels like to play. We come to think of it as optional, something we might fit in when life doesn't feel chaotic or we aren't struggling so much.

Medical doctor and psychiatrist Stuart Brown, who has done extensive research on the subject of play and is the founder of the National Institute for Play, would disagree. "I have found that remembering what play is all about and making it part of our daily lives are probably the most important factors in being a fulfilled human being," Brown wrote. "The ability to play is critical not only to being happy, but also to sustaining social relationships."[1]

Play is an essential part of a healthy life—and of a healthy marriage. Without it, we simply can't flourish.

How We View Play

Many of us do not prioritize play because it was dismissed, ignored, or minimized in our families of origin. Maybe it was a privilege allowed only after chores, work, and school, or it was seen as frivolous, so there was never time. It may have involved arguing and fighting, perhaps even leading to harm or abuse. So, naturally, today we avoid it as a form of self-protection.

Pause for a moment and ask, *How was play modeled for me? What were the messages around play?* Often, those early messages inform our hesitancy or ambivalence to play in our marriages.

My parents had a volatile relationship. As I've said, my mother leaned on me for emotional comfort because my father was often physically and emotionally unavailable, and I learned to escape through play. I'd go fishing or biking, I'd skateboard or shoot hoops, I'd juggle or walk on stilts. Play helped me cope with the relational dynamic in my home. If you're like me, you may have learned, even subconsciously, that play was a strategic way of honoring your body's need to be soothed and comforted.

Typically, play is foundational in the early months of dating. I often ask couples, "How did you play early in your relationship?"

My clients Sarah and Zeke responded to this question with delight. Zeke's face lit up as he turned toward Sarah and said, "Those were some good days. We used to hike together for hours."

She smiled and moved closer to him, saying, "Nothing mattered except being together."

"And how do you play together now?" I asked.

"We don't play," Zeke quickly answered. "I've asked her to play cards with me several times over the past few months, but each time she has said no."

Why had Sarah refused?

I eventually learned that she'd been frustrated with Zeke's work demands and his lack of emotional presence. She'd felt hurt that spending time with her had become less of a priority for him.

Sometimes the ambivalence to play is rooted in unresolved hurt.

Other times, we are simply distracted with the busyness of life. Work, chores, appointments, children, pets; play quickly slides down the list of priorities. We see little value in it, especially if we are driven by productivity and results.

Let's think about play from a child's perspective for a moment. The primary way a child feels connected to a parent is through play. If the parent is repeatedly unavailable to play, the child can internalize the parent's unavailability as a reflection of the child's worth. A lack of play is a form of misattunement and contributes significantly to shame. The child might assume, *I must not be that important. I must not matter.*

Similarly, when our partners refuse to play, dismiss our desires to play, or are consistently unavailable, we can internalize a message of shame. *I must not be that important. I must not matter.* Play communicates to our partners that they are chosen, remembered, and desired. It is a powerful antidote to shame. It helps rewrite the internal scripts our partners may be rehearsing.

When we feel frustrated or disconnected in our marriages, we often don't have much desire for play. We might think, *Why would I want to? What difference would it make?* Even if we do have some connection through play, we may not consider it to be all that beneficial; we don't sense any change or immediate results.

Rarely, though, does anything helpful or kind to our bodies produce an immediate benefit. If we take a vitamin or probiotic once, there will be no sudden change. If we are consistent with it, though, we will sense something good taking place over time.

Play is crucial to intimacy. When we aren't intentional about incorporating it into our lives together, we rob our marriages of the nutrients they need. While a relationship might go on surviving without play, it will not flourish.

Amendment to Our Soil

A few years ago, I went to a nursery to purchase a couple hydrangeas. A saleswoman asked me, "Do you need any amendments for your soil?"

After I described our hard clay soil to her, she said, "An amendment will help loosen that clay soil and provide some needed nutrients."

That sounded great, but I was in a hurry and told her, "No thanks."

At home, I hastily planted the hydrangeas without the amendment— which I now clearly see was a mistake. The hydrangeas are surviving but not flourishing. They don't have the growth or color of other hydrangeas in our yard that I later planted with an amendment.

Like the hydrangeas, we can live without the amendment of play, but we won't thrive, and we'll be more susceptible to stress and seasonal changes. Play is the amendment to our soil.

We also can think of it as the fertilizer of our soil. This past spring,

I fertilized two rows of blueberry bushes, then I ran out of fertilizer and never ended up treating a third row. While the bushes without the fertilizer did produce fruit, the bushes with the treatment yielded far more.

Jesus once told a parable about a man who looked at a fig tree in his vineyard and found no fruit on it. Hastily, he decided the tree should be chopped down (a conclusion I've often come to in my own garden).

But the caretaker of the vineyard pleaded, "Let me dig around it and fertilize it" (Luke 13:8). Essentially, "Let me tend to it more and give it the care it needs." He suggested checking back in *a year* to see if there was fruit.

Marriage is the tree that needs fertilizer to flourish, and play is the fertilizer. It's the manure, the good stuff that's vital for growth. But it won't necessarily feel easy or appealing. It will take effort, patience, and hope.

Pastor and scholar Eugene Peterson wrote this insightful reflection on this parable, and specifically manure:

> Manure is not a quick fix. It has no immediate results—it is going to take a long time to see if it makes any difference. If it's results that we are after, chopping down a tree is just the thing: we clear the ground and make it ready for a fresh start. We love beginnings: birthing a baby, christening a ship, the first day on a new job, starting a war. But spreading manure carries none of the exhilaration. It is not dramatic work, not glamorous work, not work that gets anyone's admiring attention. Manure is a slow solution. Still, when it comes to doing something about what is wrong in the world, Jesus is best known for his fondness for the minute, the invisible, the quiet, and the slow—yeast, salt, seeds, light. And manure.[2]

The soil of our hearts is impenetrable unless we tend to it with intentional play. That is what will slowly help us establish deep roots over time and bring forth fruit.

Benefits of Play

Let's look closer at what exactly happens in us when we play.

Play is nourishment for our souls. The National Institute for Play calls it "the gateway to vitality."[3]

It strengthens our friendships with our spouses, and research shows that marriages built on friendship experience more contentment than those that are not.

It cultivates intimacy—which, as we've said, means "to make known." We make ourselves known in play. It fosters emotional connection as we send the message, *I want to be with you. You matter,* and *We matter.* It's no wonder Stuart Brown has called play "the purest expression of love."[4]

This connection increases our sense of safety as we reassure our spouses that we want to stay close. Our actions say, *I choose you,* and *I choose us.*

Play also releases chemical responses in our bodies—oxytocin (which helps regulate emotions) and dopamine (which is associated with pleasure). This is no surprise. There is pleasure when we play!

It can be a healing balm, even an antibiotic, when we feel dysregulated or disconnected. Sometimes when I'm working therapeutically with a couple, I'll write a "prescription" for them: *Play three times a week for fifteen minutes.*

Here are a few simple examples of play:

- Reading aloud from a book
- Playing a game
- Meeting at a coffee shop or restaurant
- Cooking a meal
- Listening to music
- Learning a new activity

If we incorporate movement in our play, we'll experience even more benefits. Movement helps regulate us, even when trauma is activated or triggered. It increases endorphins while lowering the stress hormone cortisol, helping us naturally release stress, anxiety, and worry. Our mood improves, and, of course, we enjoy being with each other when we aren't as grumpy.

Here are a few examples of play *involving movement*:

- Walking around the neighborhood
- Going for a hike
- Gardening
- Taking a bike ride

We might primarily think of play as a significant, all-encompassing event—a day trip to a mountain or a week at a beach—and those certainly are forms of play. But we need smaller, more frequent experiences to keep the roots of our marriages growing. Consistent play sustains us.

"Do It Again"

Years ago, when our oldest son was little, Lisa and I would take him to a waterslide park. We'd stand at the bottom of the slide while Jordan flew down and excitedly splashed into the water. He'd quickly pop back up and yell, "I wanna do it again!" Then he'd hurry back to the top for another thrill.

Play is what we want to do again. What do you want to do again? What brings you joy and excitement?

Also consider: when do you find delight in your partner being playful? As I've said, watching Lisa scale the cliff brought me delight. Watching Dan catch a fish on a Montana river has brought me just as much joy as when I caught one myself. How do you enter into your partner's world of play? Is there room to watch and engage? What do you notice on your partner's face, and how does it affect you?

It's easy to underestimate the impact of honoring and taking pleasure in the other's enjoyment. While it is fun, it is not just about having fun. When Lisa watches me play in a pickleball tournament, she feels tremendous joy, and the delight I see on her face is intoxicating. This sense of connection is a gift to me.

It is especially meaningful since I rarely had that experience with my parents early in my story. It's one of the moments that reminds me we are the *face of God* to our spouses. His face reveals delight when he watches us. So when our partners delight in us, we get to sense his joy, and it is life-giving.

Rhythm of Rituals

Most evenings, Lisa and I walk our long driveway, which takes about fifteen minutes. (Like I said, it is long!) Our golden retriever, Otis, loves to come with us; if he could do cartwheels out of pure joy, he would. There is such delight when he runs free. And there is typically delight when Lisa and I are simply together walking. There is no agenda, no complicated logistics. It is just a time to share what's going on for us, a time to reflect, to know and be known.

In the mornings, Lisa and I usually share a cup of coffee together. It has been our ritual for virtually our entire marriage. While we haven't done it every single morning, the key is that it has been *consistent*.

I love early mornings. Our house's view of the sunrise over majestic Mount Baker on a clear morning is simply stunning. Today when I rose and started making coffee for the two of us, I was reminded of the beauty surrounding us and struck by the simplicity of our morning ritual; we sip coffee, offer each other presence, and notice goodness. Later, as we sat in front of the fireplace with our coffee, we paused and prayed a prayer of gratitude for the goodness of the moment.

A ritual often stirs up gratitude, as it reminds us that we are seen and chosen and that God delights in rhythms of repeated goodness.

Theologian and novelist G. K. Chesterton pondered this when he wrote:

Because children have abounding vitality, because they are in spirit fierce and free, therefore they want things repeated and unchanged. They always say, "Do it again," and the grown-up person does it again until he is nearly dead. For grown-up people are not strong enough to exult in monotony. But perhaps God is strong enough to exult in monotony. It is possible that God says every morning, "Do it again" to the sun, and every evening, "Do it again" to the moon. It may not be an automatic necessity that makes all daisies alike; it may be that God makes every daisy separately but has never got tired of making them. It may be that He has the eternal appetite of infancy, for we have sinned and grown old, and our Father is younger than we.[5]

While we can only wonder whether God creates every daisy separately, we do know that he took great delight in creating. That was, in a sense, a form of play. And we, as his image bearers, have been created to play and to enjoy rhythms of goodness.

Doing activities repeatedly together reinforces the heart posture of, *I choose you. I am with you.* That consistency of emotional presence strengthens our connection. It's why the simplest rituals can carry meaning; they establish a predictability that soothes, a structure that regulates, a reliability that reassures.

In my most recent session with Sarah and Zeke, they excitedly shared how they had been intentionally connecting for ten minutes every day.

"I feel important," Sarah said enthusiastically. "I feel like I matter."

They both said they felt more connected and that the repetition seemed to make the most impact.

Integrating more play into your relationship will require intentionality and might feel like a disruption at first. That is to be expected with anything new. Choose to prioritize it because you want to choose closeness with your partner.

When you do, you'll be embracing a change agent: the *intention to bless*. In simple ways, you'll take in the presence of your spouse with wonder, delight, and gratitude. In everyday moments, you'll be saying "heaven, yes" to the beauty you can create together.

So start to consider what you can do together repeatedly. How could you have consistent experiences of connection, even in short windows of time?

Here are some examples of rhythms and rituals:

- Sitting on the porch watching the sunset
- Doing a few yoga stretches
- Praying for each other
- Having a glass of wine before dinner

Ask yourself, What are a few ways we can begin to integrate a consistent ritual? What's something that feels doable to start with?

Remember, it can be incredibly simple, and there's really no agenda. It is about simply being in the presence of each other.

It's a ritual of presence. It communicates, *You matter*, and *We matter*.

It's a ritual of loyalty. It says to your partner, *I choose you*.

And it's a ritual of remembering your togetherness. *Let me remind you: I'm here with you.*

A Note from Lisa

I love taking walks with Steve and drinking coffee together in the morning. Our play rituals give us permission to pause from the logistics, schedules, needs, and tensions that press in. To step away from our distracted world and be present with ourselves and with each other. To relax into our bodies, be close, and connect.

In our virtual and cerebral culture, play reminds us that we are embodied. It also relieves us from the relentless pressure to be productive, freeing us to do an activity with no intended outcome and *simply feel alive*. As a weight lifts from our bodies and hearts, we feel lighter and more vibrant.

Sometimes our play involves invigorating movement, like hiking and climbing; other times it's simply about soothing calmness. We may be childlike and loud with laughter as we're watching a movie or feel an intimate silence as we're side by side playing double solitaire.

I will confess, I've been the more hesitant "player" in our relationship. I've often felt limited by how highly my family of origin valued productivity. The mantra was, *When the work is done, then—and only then—you can play.* When I started dating Steve, I was intrigued and attracted to his playful spirit as he invited me into a liminal space where we lost all track of time. We could be together for hours and not even be aware of how we spent the time. All we knew was that we felt more alive and connected.

I wonder why it is so easy to engage in play when we are dating, and then a few years into marriage, it seems impossible to set aside the time. We slip into neglecting it, overlooking its value. But, just as Steve described in his analogy of amendments and manure, prioritizing play makes an immensely positive impact over time. Long-term benefits come when we integrate these intentional moments.

As a child, my experiences with play often took place outside my home. It was an escape from the structure, duty, and expectation of performance of my family. I felt valued, noticed, and seen in play with others. Play became a form of attunement that I longed for and a way to cope with my loneliness.

Today, when I play with Steve, I am reminded, *I am not alone. I have value. I am chosen and desired.* When he texts me, "Let's go for a walk," or "Let's go grab dinner," I am grounded. As he chooses to give his full attention to me, I feel seen, known, and loved. And when we're focused on being together, nothing else matters. It is a moment in time when all that matters is *us*.

Sometimes Steve and I have gotten stuck in disagreement about what to do in play, or we've been hesitant because we've felt hurt by the other. But we've learned that sometimes we need to play out of *holy defiance*. There have been times we've driven to our favorite walking path in silence and been at odds for part of the walk. But eventually our movement helped open the door to curiosity and wonder, which then helped us open our hearts to each other.

Before we got married thirty-seven years ago, a wise mentor advised us to "steal" weekends away to build our connection. So early in our marriage, we spent a couple long weekends each year on the Oregon coast. Our rituals on those trips developed muscle memory that became embedded in our daily life together. The endless beach walks created space to listen and be curious, to wonder and dream together. Conversations over good food created a sense of deep connection and intimacy.

Playing together in our marriage makes me feel known and loved. It

A NOTE FROM LISA

provides the restorative reassurance that I am not alone; he is with me. And as we continue the rituals and stay in the rhythms of play, it makes us stronger. It softens tensions and eases repair in conflict. It helps close distance and even heal hurts. It tells us, *We are on the same team. We are for each other. We are choosing each other.*

fourteen

Blessing, Not Cursing

Dan

Love recognizes no barriers. It jumps hurdles, leaps fences,
penetrates walls to arrive at its destination full of hope.

MAYA ANGELOU

Last night held one of the darkest interactions I've had with Becky in a long while. It began with a remark about our empty refrigerator.

On many previous occasions, I had named that an empty refrigerator triggered memories of my mother's reluctance to buy groceries or fix meals. My childhood was spent with Swanson TV dinners as the best meal of the year—apart from Thanksgiving, when my father would create a sumptuous one-of-a-kind meal. Becky and I had walked through some of those memories and we both thought it was "resolved." It wasn't.

We were about to embark on a six-day trip, and Becky didn't want any extra food sitting in our refrigerator and spoiling while we were away. I had just returned from a joyous fishing trip when I discovered our impoverished supply.

"Why don't we have enough food for dinner or for breakfast tomorrow morning?" I asked her. My question was more of an accusation than a curious inquiry, holding a nuance of, *What were you thinking? Why would you put us in this position?*

There is likely nothing I could have said that would have triggered her more. She highly values preparing food well because her mother prioritized serving lavish and abundant meals; it was the only way Becky experienced love from her mother. My critical words about our food supply lit a fuse; what followed was a gas fire.

Becky glared at me and hotly demanded, "If you're starving, then why don't you look in the freezer?"

"Yes, I know there's food in the freezer," I countered. "But I'm wondering, when are we going to get food on our return home?"

This set her off. With a terse, condescending tone, she said I was unreasonable and hypersensitive, that I was unjustly criticizing her. Her anger fueled what felt like a barrage of attacks.

"Stop, please," I pleaded. "Don't treat me this way."

This only seemed to incite her more, and, with an icy face, she repeated the demand that I do a survey of what was in the freezer.

Only a year before, we had stood in front of the refrigerator in a similar but less volatile conversation, and Becky had said, "You grew up in a kind of crack house, where you were always uncertain about what you would eat. You have food insecurity."

She named what I knew to be true but had not allowed myself to own.

My mother weighed less than a hundred pounds and ate a small bowl of cereal for breakfast, a half sandwich for lunch, and a bowl of Campbell's soup for dinner. I usually ate a Swanson's TV dinner. On the rare occasions that she would cook, she served warmed-up peas and corn from cans and poorly cooked ham. This would prompt me to return to TV dinners as if they were gourmet food.

It was as if Becky had forgotten about our prior discussion or, worse, was using it against me. I had to deal not only with my story that was shameful but also the added salt in the wound of Becky's retaliation.

We were in a freefall, and every attempt to pull the rip cord left us spiraling more out of control. As the plunge accelerated, tears stung my eyes, and what I said next startled me.

"I don't need you to fix the problem. I just need you to hear me."

I have heard hundreds of women say these exact words during marriage therapy; I don't recall ever hearing a man say them. I hadn't spoken them throughout forty-seven years of marriage. The rush of panic and desperation I felt was exceedingly new, yet also ancient.

Becky and I then separated for at least a half hour.

To my surprise, flashes of memory bombarded me. I saw my eight-year-old self huddled in a corner, holding my toy dachshund, trying to escape my mom's rage and cope with my distress of the inevitable food scarcity in our home.

I had a choice to make: Would I turn away from this hurting boy? Would I rage against Becky? Or would I simply shut down?

I resolved not to battle Becky and not to withdraw. I turned toward the boy; I engaged what was raging in me.

What occurred next shocked me. Eight-year-old Danny, already significantly overweight, awkward, and lonely, could not lift his head and meet my eyes. I could see my fear of not having access to bodily nourishment, my distress from having unmet needs, and my anguish from facing my mom's contempt. They were crushing this boy, and they were at the root of my reaction to an empty refrigerator.

The present war with Becky faded as I realized that the bigger war I was fighting was with myself. While I would need to reengage with her soon, that was not the first order of concern. I needed to bless a brokenhearted young boy. Then I could seek to bless Becky.

Every marriage is a tapestry of two lives, each bringing threads of different ages and events, and they all are joined together in a rough weave.

In an instant, I was thrown into the dark "backside" of our marriage and of my life. We all have versions of these moments, and it is in these points that we make a critical decision.

Will we bless or curse?

Will we bless our unhealed, unredeemed younger selves, or will we curse them? Will we extend love or resentment, grace or harm, care or cruelty?

This choice sets into motion whether we will bless or curse the one who has brought these parts to the surface.

I wish I could tell you that the process I took to bless my younger self and my wife was rapid and elegant. It was not. The internal war, if one avoids a cowardly surrender and escape, is typically messy.

As Becky retreated to take a bath, I lay down in bed. I could feel the roiling seduction to make a vow.

I will never, never ever share with her that I feel scared.

I will never let anyone humiliate me again, ever.

I will never let food be a war again.

It was like standing in the ocean and being knocked down by one wave, only to stand, and be knocked down by another. The words in my mind crashed, and I was in one instant enraged and then ashamed.

As I looked back at the terrified eight-year-old, I knew that if I cursed him, I would curse Becky. And if I cursed her and made those vows, I would be cursing myself and, ultimately, God. The process of choosing whether to bless or curse is messy and jagged, but there are moments when the choice is simple.

Let me state a premise that is hard to swallow. There is no neutrality in the matter of blessing or cursing. We either bless or curse—there is no middle ground. We either are moving toward each other for the sake of the wild, inconceivable glory of God, or we are not.

Most moments in a marriage—cutting the lawn, taking out the garbage, cleaning up dog poop, driving kids to school, paying bills—feel inevitable and uneventful. They are not instances when the choice to bless or curse feels relevant.

It is at moments of adversity and extremity that the question is most crucial. If it doesn't come into our purview, we will simply cope to survive and minimize pain. While this will feel natural and harmless, it is unwittingly joining the kingdom of evil.

The kingdom of evil wants judgment and division. It fosters disdain justified by heartache and the loss of hope. It is subtle until it is not.

Amid days that are busy and unpredictable because hell has rent the surface, the stance you take toward yourself and your spouse will determine your future.

The days ahead, however, will not be darkened by the first round of cursing or even in the first dozen vows. It is a cumulative effect occurring over countless interactions, to the point where something in your heart deadens and gives up desire through the numbing of pain. The vows of cursing you've made are like plaque that slowly thickens the arteries unnoticed until the heart stops beating.

Divorce is not when the heart stops; it is when the body is buried. The heart stopped well before—sometimes decades before—the papers are signed.

Perhaps as tragic, many remain married in a frozen state of perceived normalcy, starved and emaciated through denial and neglect. When a good marriage is conceived as conviviality, few tensions, and shared interests, it is hard to make the power of blessing vivid.

That is, until we remember our marriage vows.

Vows of Promissory Blessing

We make vows at the outset of our union to envision how we will shape our future together. What will our story be? It will include good times and tough days. Health and illness. Loss of time, energy, finances, and eventually our earthly life. But above all, true togetherness, affection, and loyalty. We set out to write not every event, but the story of how we will *be with* each other amid the twists and turns.

How often do you think about the vows you spoke many moons ago?

It is rare even to remember what we promised our partners on our wedding days. It is like the day we got a diploma. Do we remember the lovely, inspirational speech or even who gave it? Ceremonies inaugurate, but they fade as the labor demands focus. Few even frame their degrees, let alone their vows. We don't invest much stock in a vow, yet it is our North Star.

Let me remind you of a traditional wedding vow.

"In the name of God, I, [name], take you, [name], to be my wife/husband, to have and to hold from this day forward, for better, for worse, for richer, for poorer, in sickness and in health, to love and to cherish, until we are parted by death. This is my solemn vow."

I personally love the brevity and clarity of a traditional Celtic vow.

"You are blood of my blood, bone of my bone. I give you my body, that we might be one. I give you my spirit, until our life is done."

A vow is an oath that implies a blood sacrifice. In an ancient covenantal ceremony, the two who were binding their hearts together would cut their flesh, symbolizing the merging of their blood and bone. Drinking wine at a covenantal meal represented the same. *Your life is mine to protect and honor, just as my life is your treasure.*

Marriage vows are an oath of loyalty that say, "I will shed blood for you, sorrow with you in your losses, and celebrate with you your victories. And if need be, I will die with you and for you."

In the analogy of gardening, making this vow involves furrowing the ground—cutting into it to prepare it to grow life-giving fruit. We break open the hard, compacted soil so it can receive the nutrients, amendments, and seed that will bring a rich harvest. In a marriage vow, we purpose to give ourselves, but we also cut ourselves open to "furrow the ground," to receive what the other is meant to give.

This is how we begin to bless. We open ourselves with the intent to give and receive. It is infinitely more, but no less, than allowing our words to bind us to our beloved to create goodness.

It is the antithesis to a curse.

Vows of Deterministic Cursing

A curse *cuts your partner*, making them pay for your failure and pain, and provides an escape from suffering the furrowing of your soul. It is a judgment, a stance of contempt, that freezes the other in the pronouncement that there is nothing good to be enjoyed.

"You are such an idiot."

"You will never change."

"You don't think about anyone or anything other than yourself."

"You ruin everything I try to do."

"You are a liar."

"You will never tell the truth."

"You are such a bully."

"You are such a coward."

"Go to hell!"

What we must not miss is that we can just as often turn curses against ourselves or allow the cursing of others to remain in us.

A teacher who tells you directly or indirectly you are stupid has given you a curse. A parent who tells you that you are making a fool out of yourself as you sing your heart out in a plastic microphone has given you a curse. To be told as a woman to tone down your intensity because it might make a man feel uncomfortable is a curse.

We know the person that gives us a finger as we are driving or attacks us for how we are wearing our hair is cursing us. We know what it means when someone uses curse words to infect us. But do we know slower, more normalized cursing, when we privately make vows to keep ourselves safe from each other?

When the tension of my fight with Becky led me to tuck into bed as she was taking a bath, I grappled with cursing her by making a vow that I would never let her make me feel bad about food and our refrigerator again. I am grateful I was working on this concept of blessing and cursing at the time, and that it dawned on me that I was nearing both cursing my eight-year-old self and my wife. It took longer than I wished, but I ultimately resolved to cut the curse, furrow the soil of my heart, and return to my covenantal blood promise.

I had to orient my heart back to Becky, despite my hurt and the sense of injustice I felt in her response.

I will not condemn and curse.

I will not make a final judgment on myself or on her.

I will not form a cocoon of condemnation that soothes me but poisons our love.

I will not perpetuate pain and close us off to goodness.

A curse settles the future with an unbending, never-ending finality. There is no room for change and growth. If a blessing is like a verdant, green garden that prepares for growing good fruit, a curse is an arid, bone-dry desert that settles for certainty that nothing can possibly grow. A curse scorches the earth and dumps contaminating chemicals that poison the ground. A blessing makes way for lavish goodness, daring to hope for beauty and newness.

It is imperative to remember: there is no neutrality. Daily we either curse ourselves and our spouses, or we bless.

To put it more starkly: if you are not actively blessing, you are unwittingly cursing. Operating in a marriage as if someone or something else is at the wheel and all you need to do is "just live life" sets you up for a movement toward cursing. It is a drastic contrast from what you originally set out to do in the beginning of your life together.

The Cultivation of Blessing

As we've said, it is likely you don't remember your vows. No worries. Whatever your vows were a dozen years ago, or five decades ago, they need to be rewritten. How sweet would it be to take time to write out what you promise to each other today?

Blessing begins with words. Simply writing the words *I take and hold you* is a left-frontal-lobe move that activates the body to move.

How will you move?

Consider a picture from our backyard garden as you think on it.

We have four raised beds that are ten feet by four feet, giving us 160 square feet to work with. I divide the beds into square-foot farming. Carrots get sixteen seeds per square foot and squash gets one per square foot. Becky loves to have flowers in every bed, and we finally got a trellis to let climbing plants do their thing.

We test the soil, we water and weed, and we snatch snails and other critters out of the bed. There are foxes that will take down a vineyard. There are vines that bear no fruit. There is pruning for all branches, or the fruit will not grow as we dream. We don't merely plant seeds and then go harvest fruit. It takes work. It takes knowledge and determination. It takes intention.

It is the same with the approach we take to our relational dynamic.

I love the Celtic vow because it is short and it rhymes, so I can memorize it and regularly use it as a compass. I have begun saying it to Becky when we walk every morning as we talk and pray. "You are blood of my blood, bone of my bone. I give you my body, that we might be one. I give you my spirit, until our life is done." It sets up our day to walk into the garden to water, dig, and pull. It scatters the clouds of busyness that make me myopic and dull. It is not a panacea—nothing is—but it helps me, even momentarily, to focus early in the morning on what I want to be most true about how I live.

To bless my beloved, however, I must become beloved.

Or perhaps truer said, I must *enter how beloved I am.*

This requires daily attention to how much I believe God when I recall the psalmist's words: "How precious are your thoughts about me, O God. They cannot be numbered" (Psalm 139:17 NLT).

This is not merely an act of self-validation highlighting our best qualities. If it were, it would ring true but have no more substance than a Hallmark card. It is an acceptance of our real selves as we listen to the only one who sees *all* of us and can say with authority whether we are lovable. Even acceptable. We, the broken, look in a mirror from him and see ourselves positively covered with his grace, adoration, and delight.

Even if we get to this point, we may miss the critical next step: to become a sponge to his abundant love for us, letting it fully saturate us, all the way down to our deepest, darkest places.

And we must be aware of those places if we are to let him reach us there.

This requires addressing questions such as, Who has cursed me, and how have I joined the cursing against me? Further, who has envied me and wished harm for what they perceive to be my privileges? How have I internalized that?

There are reasons we find it hard to embrace the delight of God. Perhaps the most central reason is that we know we fail and—far more than making mistakes—our hearts can be cold, hard, and mean. Which is another way to say: we all struggle with sin.

I curse. Often. Not merely with so-called curse words but with language shaded (or packed to the gills) with contempt. But someone has borne the consequences of all my cursing and, despite my contempt, still pursues, delights in, and honors me.

I can't allow myself to be blessed until I feel this truth in my bones. I can't know how precious I am until I grasp how enormously someone has sacrificed to invite me back to relationship. Our grasp of being loved will change over many seasons and years, and what we knew in the past will seem paltry to what we know now. Yet what we know now is a small foretaste of what is ahead.

I have known that blood sacrifice in how Becky has loved me despite my failures. I have offered her that grace as well. And we are simply offering to each other what Jesus has offered to us.

The apostle Paul spoke of Jesus' mind-bending sacrifice in these terms: "Christ redeemed us from the curse of the law by becoming a curse for us, for it is written: 'Cursed is everyone who is hung on a pole.'

He redeemed us in order that the blessing given to Abraham might come to the Gentiles through Christ Jesus, so that by faith we might receive the promise of the Spirit" (Galatians 3:13–14).

Someone greater than us took our curse and cursing, every failure of love, and bore the cost to free us from the weight of our sin. It is a gift we receive, one I get to offer to my beloved and one she can offer to me.

Do I deserve to be forgiven? Do I deserve not to be cursed and not held fully and completely accountable for every failure?

Absolutely not.

But I am.

I am forgiven in the heavenlies, in the unseen realm. And I am forgiven among our backyard trees, flowers, and vegetables, in the seen realm.

As my beloved and I bless and forgive each other, our garden is growing. We are inviting more life, goodness, and beauty to come in. Are there ample obstacles to overcome day after day? Yes. Nevertheless, I don't bear the curse, nor does my partner. Instead, we are covered with God's blessing. So we tend to our ground, and then we sit, eat, drink, laugh, cry, and honor the presence of God in each other.

Every evening meal is a celebration at the end of a day of struggle. Those struggles may be the minor irritations of commuting or that we ran out of ketchup. They may involve warfare so severe that it drains our reserves and flattens our hope. But if we can sit across from each other at the table, and, even for a few moments, look at the precious gift of the other, we have something to celebrate.

Daily Inviting More Life and Goodness

As we close this chapter, let's return to a fundamental truth: *We are meant for honor and delight.* To receive it, to give it. To live it and be shaped by it. And who is the ultimate source of it? Our tender God, who is Love.

There are days when we are determined to keep our hearts locked up tight, forcing ourselves to be completely closed off from him. No blessing comes in or out. No becoming beloved. No soaking up grace and adoration down to our core. We perceive it as self-protection, but it will ensnare us in the misery of cursing and align us with the evil of judgment, division, and disdain.

We can start to loosen up those locks on our hearts by getting curious.

In what ways am I more accustomed to cursing than blessing?

Why do I find it hard to embrace the delight of God?

What aspects of myself or my story do I assume make me unlovable to him?

Explore this deeply and fully. But also know that no human heartache, shame, or hopelessness can override the character of God. Your failures cannot stop his pursuing love or change the extravagant sacrifice he made to lift your curse and bring you close.

Invite your partner into your curiosity and exploration. It is a brave thing to be honest about your humanity and to choose intimacy—and a life-giving and strengthening thing. A marriage, after all, is far more than a convenience or a mere comfort; it is a bastion against despair and a rampart to protect us from our enemies.

Marriage is a feast celebrating the wonder that love wins over hate and a proclamation that death never gets the final word. It is a song that enables us to sing of our divine Beloved who has taken the curse that we might bless each other.

A marriage is a vow spoken to each other and whispered to God, which helps us refuse to curse so we can participate in the blessing of God's banquet of delight.

This is what he is making available to you in your marriage today. Will you enter the feast? Will you sing the song?

These are, no doubt, grand, epic concepts—and yet they are livable. We move toward them through daily choices and intentions.

Assess where you are. How much intentional blessing or unwitting cursing might currently exist in your marriage?

Consider where you want to go. What do you want to be most true about how you live? What vow do you want to shape your future, and how could you take time together to reset yourselves toward it?

Lean into the change agents of defiance and the intention to bless.

In *defiance*, you refuse to allow hurt, anger, and past failure to determine the future of what you are able to create together. You take a stance of "hell, no" to death and evil in all its forms.

With *the intention to bless*, you hold each other with wonder, awe, delight, and gratitude. You take a stance of "heaven, yes" to the beauty and goodness you can create together.

Picture the moments when you'll be tempted to curse yourself or your partner. Imagine what it might mean to open yourself more to give and receive life.

To furrow the soil of your heart and return to your blood covenantal promise.

To remind your partner of the sacrifice of Jesus and his outrageous forgiveness.

To water their soul with God's grace, adoration, and delight.

To let echoes of his heart ring out to them: You are my beloved. I am yours; you are mine. I know you deeply. And I choose to bless you, always.

A Note from Becky

I t is crazy how our refrigerator conflict escalated into high-alert ferocity! On one hand, it's hard to imagine how we ended up there. But on the other, our past stories were clearly playing out in the present, and we were bearing the combined impact of extensive travel, sorrow from loss, and grating physical ailments. Dan was struggling to hear, and, after a recent surgery, I was having trouble speaking. Talk about striving to maintain attunement. Truly, Jesus had our attention.

Facing our past stories that have shaped us is never easy, at least for Dan and me. As he sat with his terrified eight-year-old self, hurting from his mother's rage and neglect, I was stuck in my own story. I had received Dan's remarks about the state of our refrigerator—an area of our life I considered my domain—as an attack, and I felt a determined fury to protect myself. I was living out what I'd experienced a thousand times in my family of origin.

In a sense, I became an enemy to him. And it was in the exact moment I should have joined him in tending to his wounded younger self.

We needed a counselor. A referee. The Holy Spirit. We needed help navigating our hurt and embracing the healing process together.

But instead of seeking that help, we each sought safety in going separate directions, and there was no repair that night.

As Dan went to bed and I took a bath, I fluctuated between making vows against him and trusting his perspective that I was being unkind. Then memories from our early years flooded back to me, moments when he'd found fault with my parents and asked me to see things from his perspective. Before I knew it, I was back in time with my twenty-five-year-old self, feeling desperate to protect my family and myself. As I sunk deeper into the waters of hurt, I wound up feeling caught in a tsunami of defensiveness.

It seemed so ridiculous that a refrigerator would derail us like that. *He's being such a baby*, I kept thinking. *He needs to grow up and notice he hasn't starved so far.*

I won't let his struggle be my fault.

Every time I repeated these sentences, I felt secure but cold and enraged.

I vowed not to take the blame for our derailed evening. I always put effort into organizing our food—and not in a way to instill fear in him. The fact he can't see that is his problem. Digging in my heels, I chose to see the log in his eye and no speck in mine.

My sleep was anything but restorative.

By the next morning, however, I'd come to realize that my stance against Dan had been condescending. I had, in fact, been in the wrong. As he was still sleeping, I drank coffee and dreaded acknowledging this to him.

Apologizing always makes me feel foolish and young, because I constantly had to stand up for myself in my early years. Defensiveness was my oxygen—my method for enduring the harm in my home. Showing vulnerability goes against how I learned to live as a child. Staying guarded is how I feel strong; it's how I have survived in this crazy world.

Amid my struggle, words from my therapist came to mind: When you are in distress, see if you can narrate what is happening in you.

There were so many things happening inside of me; it was chaos. I realized I needed to address it on my own, notice all I could about it, and talk through it.

It was frightening to make space for *me*—the good, the bad, and the ugly—as it always is. But I chose to do it, even as I felt the fear. I asked questions of my soul, then took time to hear what was inside.

Is my defensiveness really protecting me?

If I quit defending myself, will I find peace or humiliation?

Can I trust Dan's love for me?

My inner dialogue began to shift away from blaming Dan and even to owning my fault in the matter. It was as if the Spirit joined the conversation with my soul without speaking a single word; he simply quieted my heart and body, enough for me to *feel* the impact of our conflict and grasp a bigger perspective. I became viscerally aware of our individual and shared stories, which finally overpowered any sense of threat. I just felt sad about Dan's heartache and our division.

By the time Dan walked into the kitchen, I didn't want to defend, turn away, or hide. These were the early shoots of spring flowers breaking the surface in my heart.

We took our routine morning walk, and I apologized. The particular words I used were not as important as the posture of softness, compassion, and kindness I brought him. I finally wanted to enter his heartache more than I wanted to be free from my shame. I longed to truly bless him—to give him something life-giving and good. And my apology opened the door for me to give him the greatest blessing I could: a true desire to know what he feared and to be with him in it.

I came to the conversation ready to address the log in my own eye, then Dan did something that made the process easier. He took my hand in his before we even began to walk.

It is a mystery to me how hearts come back together. I know I had a part. I know his taking my hand eased the first few words. But what feels truer is that the Spirit had been interceding for us and brought us both to the desire not to curse, but to bless.

fifteen

Coming to the Banquet of Delight

Dan

I asked myself, why do I love, and what is the power of
beauty, and I understood that each and every instance
of beauty is a promise and example, in miniature,
of life that can end in balance, with symmetry,
purpose, and hope—even if without explanation.

MARK HELPRIN

The most intriguing vows I've ever heard were at a wedding I officiated with a friend.

The groom, a brilliant and playful musician and poet, spoke of his love and gratitude to have found a woman whose gifting and eccentricities accented and disrupted his way of being in the world. He was elegant and swift, devoted and honoring.

The bride, a superb theologian, pastor, and spiritual director, offered a lovely, enriching contemplation. It was essentially a mini sermon, involving a quote she read from a thick theological tome that summarized her passion to bring flourishing and goodness to his life.

I could see the audience reflecting my own holy amusement, brilliant joy, and resounding *yes*. We were seeing them in their compelling uniqueness. His vows shimmered like the gold leaves of an aspen grove. Her vows were profound, dense, and deeply rooted in theological dirt.

Before my friend and I pronounced them husband and wife, I encouraged the audience members who were married to take on those glorious vows they'd heard as their own.

Then, a party. Blessings. Stories. Lavish food, wine, music, and dancing. It didn't feel like a religious event that had been handed off to a party; it was a banquet, a celebration that came after a long and at times arduous battle to find each other, trust, love, and join as one.

I knew their stories and the heartache they'd brought to dating. I knew the betrayals each had suffered and the immensity of their risk to love again. They had been at war with each other, with themselves, at times with their communities and friends, and certainly with the kingdom of evil. They had sustained losses in warfare and have scars that will remain. Their love had intensified their sorrow—and deepened their joy of having prevailed together.

In ancient cultures, when a battle was won, a banquet followed. It was a time to honor the living for their courageous tenacity and victory, and a time to remember the fallen, the losses on the battlefield. This wedding reception, without a doubt, mirrored that.

Their union was a communion of laughter and tears and death and resurrection, which can be said of every good marriage. And a true banquet is not just an effort to eat, drink, and be merry—a dulling of the senses through denial—but an intensification of desire to open ourselves to greater sorrow and joy.

We danced long and hard that night, with an intensity I'd seldom experienced at weddings. I think the reason was most of us knew the death that had been suffered to bring the life that was present.

We danced not merely for the event, but for the wonder that death had not won and did not have the right to claim the final word.

We danced the resurrection.

We had, after all, received a taste of what is to come. The victory and relief. The wholeness and delight. The glorious goodness and forever abundant life. We all need to party, to celebrate and enter into what our hearts most deeply desire, which is to see all forms of death destroyed.

Scripture assures us, "The LORD Almighty will prepare a feast of rich food for all peoples, a banquet of aged wine—the best of meats and the finest of wines. On this mountain he will destroy the shroud that enfolds all peoples, the sheet that covers all nations: he will swallow up death forever. The Sovereign LORD will wipe away the tears from all faces; he will remove his people's disgrace from all the earth" (Isaiah 25:6–8).

This Is the Place for Transformation

It is not likely that, at your wedding, the officiant said, "A war had to be fought for these two to be at this altar." Even more unlikely is that they'd continue, "And now, in fact, there will commence an even greater war."

Marriage is, in a sense, a microcosm of fighting the good fight of faith, of defiantly saying "hell, no" to what leads us away from God's heart and life, and of saying "heaven, yes" to the beauty and transformation he invites us to. Marriage is not merely a conflict between two people; it is a battle with every form of death that threatens to separate the couple. To fight well is to transform not only two hearts and the marriage, but also to offer hope to all who see the bounty of redemption. Every marriage is meant to do more than sustain the life of the family; it is to be a transformative gift to family, friends, neighbors, and all who encounter true honesty and hope.

After looking at this reality from different angles with you throughout this book, I will share a quote I wouldn't have asked you to consider until now. It comes from Harrison Scott Key, a brilliant professor and comedy writer. His book *How to Stay Married: The Most Insane Love Story Ever Told* is the most hilarious, agonizing, staggering marriage story I have ever read.

Key depicts his discovery of his wife's affair and his subsequent turmoil. Their tale is dark, horrifying, apocalyptic—and healing. His account is thick with irony, anger, confusion—and faith, which ultimately saved his life and marriage. His unraveling, rebuilding, and reflecting led him to write these words:

> Whatever your feelings about Christ being the bridegroom and church being the bride, here's what I've come to see: Rome slaughtered Jesus, and that's what marriage will do. It will slay you, crucify and burn and behead you and everything you thought you knew about yourself. And the thing that is left, after all is burned and plucked away, that is the real you.
>
> Marriage has changed over the millennia, and that's a beautiful thing, but the prophets of this present age would have us believe marriage should exist solely for the benefit of the people in it, for their emotional, psychological, and carnal empowerment, as though matrimony is merely an extended couple's spa experience featuring orgies and explosive self-actualizations that you can exit whensoever your heart desires. What if the prophets are wrong? Are we not freer than ever in human history, and sadder and more anxious, more wretched? What if marriage, at its very best, exists to remake us into beautiful new creatures we scarcely recognize? What if, in some cosmically weird way, escaping a hard marriage is not how you change? What if staying married is?[1]

This is a far cry from a recommendation that we merely survive a difficult marriage or endure a tedious dynamic. It instead is a challenge to a self-deluded warrior who has discovered that it is only the weak, foolish, and needy who plunge into the turbulent waters of redemption—a place where you risk drowning but also is your only hope for rescue. No matter what occurs, the guarantee is you will not come out the person you were. And even more, the promise is that you will become who you could not have imagined you would be.

This is why we can't eat and drink and dance well at the party if we fail to struggle with what Scripture described above—the veil of death, the tears not yet bottled, the "disgrace" that remains with us. Wrestling with these realities is, as dramatic as it may seem, an almost daily task. Death, tears, and shame are near the surface every day, and at times burst into full view.

Displaying Brokenness Captured by Love

One Sunday I asked Becky, "Is there anything you'd like to do today that we could do together?"

She jumped at my offer and replied, "The front yard needs weeding."

I don't mind weeding our backyard garden, but for some reason the front yard felt overwhelming. I kept this to myself and agreed.

We began the task and soon I pulled out a "weed" that was in fact a perennial.

Becky chastened me and explained again what a weed was and what was to be left.

I listened then returned to my inexorable burden and, before long, made another error.

"Stop and *pay attention!*" Becky shouted at me.

Her words felt demeaning. I upped the ante and returned her offense with a sharp reply. "Look, I'm not a horticultural genius like you—I'm just a hired hand, so give me some latitude. Or let me just carry the manure while you weed."

She responded, "Just go watch football or write a book, but whatever you do, stop ruining my flowers."

My well-intentioned desire to be with her and honor her wishes had landed me in what felt like a maze—a labyrinth, and Becky was the minotaur.

I stood my ground against my enemy and shouted, but this time my words felt hollow and silly. I was either going to leave, shut down, or admit I was wrong. I wasn't at what some might call full repentance. Instead, I yelled, "*I am wrong. I am sorry.* I won't keep blaming you, but I don't know if I can pull weeds and not do some harm."

At my paltry confession, we were both caught off guard by loud applause that came from next door. We looked over and saw three couples, our neighbors, sitting on a porch watching us fight.

As their applause dwindled, they called for us to join them. They were drinking beer and snacking and had been watching us for a while.

At first, the jovial banter about our acrimony felt light and playful, but then one wife said to Becky, "How do you get him to apologize? Nothing seems to work with Jack."

In an instant, the tone changed.

Becky laughed and said, "As you know from living near us, Dan is an odd man. He is at times a wreck, and he knows it. I have always loved that he can name his failures without making me pay and wants to be a better man."

The tone changed even more radically.

Another wife said to me, "We all know you are a little weird, but how did you come to be able to admit you are wrong?"

The men were looking at me with a stare that said, Don't betray us. Don't sell us down the river and make our marriages any harder than they already are. Make a joke and move on.

But that is not my style.

I asked the congregation, especially looking at the men, "Do you want a two-dollar, five-dollar, or ten-dollar answer? If you want the deluxe response, give me a beer."

One of the braver men handed me a beer and said, "I want the full tour."

We began with my dropping a pencil in tenth-grade French class so I could stare at Becky's legs. We quickly wound our way to my borderline schizophrenic mother and my hatred of being needed and used to keep her alive. We covered how Becky's world forced her to be independent and need no one, and what a perfect match we were. The only problem was, Jesus had ruined both of our lives and compelled us to look at ourselves, at reality, and at the love we were created to know.

We didn't "evangelize." We simply shared our story, and it involves Jesus. We believe. We don't believe. We both know we need help.

Our story prompted conversation about how each couple had met and what they'd hoped would be redeemed in their marriage. We spoke about how we all are such staggeringly beautiful and broken creatures who long for rescue and redemption. It was a holy Sunday afternoon, drinking beer, eating Cheetos, and talking about the mystery of marriage.

This is what you and your partner can offer to your neighbors, friends, and family too.

Failing, but Still Loving

Many of us present to others only glossy half-truths of our marriage experiences. But we are people of the truth, so why don't we tell the truth? I don't mean air the so-called dirty laundry by sharing what has not been addressed in private together, perhaps with a good therapist or wise friend. I mean speaking honestly about our human experience.

We all are broken and lonely.

We all struggle to believe and trust.

We all, at some level, are resolutely independent and angry.

We all want far more delight and honor—unless we have grown numb and let our desire dim.

To the degree we can tell the truth, privately and then publicly, in wise and kind ways, we can invite others to tell the truth too. To ask them to step into their stories, engage with them fully and honestly, and imagine where they could go next. Every marriage is a complex and beautiful story that seldom gets read or spoken. The more honest we are about our stories and their origins, heartaches, and glory, the more others will be invited to engage their own.

Once we give up the illusion that others seem to have it all together—that their social media pictures tell the truth—we can turn to the ones we love and ask for more and offer more.

The *more* we offer comes from a desire to bless, not to own and control. Our marriages are not ours to possess, just as our partners, fellow image bearers, are not ours to possess. We offer an outpouring of love, and all love is a gift. It is undeserved and stems from a love that is greater than any we could conjure on our own.

But what we offer is compelling and tasty, even if it is the not-entirely-filling hors d'oeuvres that are a prelude to the full banquet. This is the inheritance we give our children, friends, family, and world.

On our twenty-fifth wedding anniversary, I asked our children to write a letter to Becky and me answering the question, *What have you learned about life from watching our marriage?* Then we all went to a restaurant and read the letters together. It is one of the richest nights in our memory.

At one point, Becky and I were crying, and the waiter, awkward and concerned, asked, "Is there any problem with the food?"

We laughed and told him that our children were talking with us about our failures and grace and what they'd learned from watching our marriage for twenty-two, eighteen, and fourteen years.

He looked at us and said to our children, "I have never heard of anything like this in my life. You all are so fortunate to have each other."

The theme that echoed throughout the evening was this: "You both fail a lot, really a lot—and Dad more than you, Mom. But you both seem to return to each other and never quit. You fight, but you still love. It makes it seem possible for a marriage to last."

Receiving His Goodness and Love Together

None of us could have imagined what we were saying when we originally spoke vows to our partners. We did not deeply know ourselves or our spouses; we had no clue what marriage would unearth.

There is a place for honoring our naivete and likely our self-righteous presumption that our marriages would be different. We would not succumb to the fighting or flee from each other like the plague. We would be honest, but generous. We would have conflict, but in the end see eye to eye. Our passion would not flicker or ever be snuffed out. We were different.

And we were.

And we were not.

Those flimsy Hollywood fronts and cardboard edifices were knocked down in the first several years, then propped back up again to look like the town we created. It didn't last. What did last was the memory of love, a remnant of delight and honor, and the conventions of normalcy that propelled us to work, school, church, and the soccer field. It was the busyness and exhaustion, the stuff in the garage, and the relentless mortgage that kept our marriage together.

Throughout this book, Steve and I have been whispering and shouting, *There is more.* More sorrow. More joy. More complexity. More clarity of purpose.

What are we most wanting for you? The answer is simple.

Bless what your spouse reveals about your need for grace.

Bless them for being the face of God and at times the smell of hell.

Stay in the conflict until you need to care for your body and your fragmenting brain.

Return and ask the question of yourself and your spouse that Steve and Lisa borrowed from God: *Where are you?*

Meaning, Where have you gone? Do you want to come back?

The goal of marriage is to convince us at the deepest recesses of our bodies and hearts that we can't remain who we are and create the world of love we desire. We are to realize that much of our present story flows from the pages of the past, but if we go back and scribble in the margins of our heartache, we can start writing a new story. If we engage the past with an eye on the future, addressing the log in our dogmatic perspectives and demands, we will be formed, as Key said, into "beautiful new creatures we scarcely recognize." We also are meant to offer others this hope of transformation and join them in the dance of redemption.

But we'll never get to step into that until we *open ourselves* to it.

It is, after all, the ones who grieve their brokenness who will rejoice in their wholeness. It's the ones who admit they need healing who will be healed. It feels counterintuitive to human nature, but it is the way of Jesus. The humble will be lifted up. The last will be first. Those who give up their lives will gain them. Jesus is all about reversal.

So, of course, he said, "When you give a banquet, invite the poor, the crippled, the lame, the blind, and you will be blessed" (Luke 14:13–14).

Do you want a deeply rooted marriage? Then come to the wedding feast broken and needy, just as those Jesus described.

As our children frankly told us, Becky and I fail; we fail a lot. We are poor, weak, and myopic at best. But we came to a banquet, even though we each were a wreck, and we were captured by a love that would not let us go. We were seized by a love that is relentless, apocalyptic, and infinitely kind.

Now, as much as we can, we offer that love to each other.

What we offer each other then becomes the fruit—the bread, meat, cheese, and wine—that we can set before you, and everyone we know, to eat. It's a lavish banquet of delights that is free to us all, because it came at the cost of another: Jesus, "the Lamb of God, who takes away the sin of the world" (John 1:29). The one who came to give us life to the full, who is now preparing for us the complete, heavenly banquet, said, "Let anyone who is thirsty come to me and drink" (7:37).

So come. Come and drink and eat.

Taste and see the goodness of God.

Receive the honor and delight he has for you.

Receive his rich fare and the privilege of supping together, which makes the battle worth the cost and the suffering worthy of joy.

Come and see a love that is bigger than you both and the new creature you each will be.

Acknowledgments

Dan

The moment I put my mind to the question, Who do I wish to thank? I was caught in a wave of nostalgia and wonder. To put it another way, Who has invested in Becky or me, and more directly in our marriage, making it possible to write this book? Countless friends have borne our dreams and nightmares and urged us never to let love die. The list is far longer than I can address here, and there is so much more to be said for each person and couple. Let this suffice:

Tremper and Alice Longman and Dave and Meg Dupee: We ripped up the slopes, wept in laughter, and somehow survived our wild post-Christmas ski trips. Longmans, you were the first to marry and give us a vision of grace in process.

Scotty and Darlene Smith: From the hallowed walls of seminary to countless conversations about life, love, and the glory of God, we have aged together and stumbled forward.

The Sailing Crew—Len and Sheri; LaJean and David; Mark and Debi: We have sailed the world with you. We have wept in the face of death, celebrated weddings, and suffered accidents, losses, and retirement. What a ride, dear friends.

John and Stasi Eldredge: So many countless nights sitting on the deck at the ranch watching the thunder and lightning while anticipating the ever-present arrival of the King. The delight of those evenings is a foretaste of what is ahead.

Steve and Lisa Call: What a dream come true to play with you. The countless trips to Montana, when we schemed, pondered, and prayed for this labor to come to be, is a majestic mark of God's faithfulness. We are so grateful for younger companions who will forge ahead over many more decades.

Our children, Annie and Driscoll, Amanda and Jeff, and Andrew and Sassy: Nothing has propelled us to love more than seeing the goodness of your marriages. Annie, Amanda, and Andrew, you made stunningly wise decisions to marry your spouses. Driscoll, Sassy, and Jeff, we love how you love our beloved children. There is no privilege in this life more incredible than witnessing your marriages and how you love your children.

Sealy Yates: As I have said in countless books, you are not merely one of a kind; you are a kind that brings oneness amid conflict and struggle. You have been far more than an agent—a mentor and friend.

Carrie Marrs: It is a crime that your name is not above ours on the masthead. As an editor and a dear friend, you have sacrificed and labored to bring the best out of us that can be found. Any errors and idiosyncrasies are ours and not yours. This book offers not merely your profound skill but the depth of your love for your husband and daughter.

Finally, my beloved friend, lover, wife, and ally, Becky: A dear friend read several chapters and said, "It is the best writing of any of your books." I hope that is true. If it is, it is only for one reason: writing about you brings more sorrow, wonder, gratitude, and joy than any other person or topic I know on this earth. No one has ever or will ever be the face of God to me as you are. I offer the simplest of words: *Thank you.*

Steve

It has truly been a gift and privilege to write this book. I remember my ninth-grade creative writing teacher, Mrs. Wicks, who encouraged me just to tell the story. And here we are. We have told the story.

Previous and current clients: You have shaped and formed me and, through our work together, helped clarify what is needed to sustain a life-giving marriage. Thank you.

Marriage small groups: Over the years, your kindness and authenticity in revealing deep places of heartache and desire in your marriages have contributed to what has been written here. Thank you.

Denny and Marilyn Rydberg: You were our first mentors early in our marriage. Your humility, kindness, and playful spirits were contagious. You offered us the blueprint of what a deep-rooted marriage could be. Thank you.

Dan and Becky Allender: It has been such a joy to play together over these past years. Years of dreaming of what could be have become a reality because you have invited us to journey with you. Thank you.

Students and graduates of the Seattle School of Theology and Psychology: For more than twenty years, you have taught me what it means to live in this world with kindness and humility. Writing this book came from your invitations to put "what you teach into a book." Thank you.

Carrie Marrs: Our esteemed editor. You are an artist and a visionary. Your fierce and playful spirit has been such a gift in this process. We could not have created this without your kind and authentic self. Thank you.

Our children, Jordan and Erica, Maddy and Alvaro, and Ellie: What a privilege it has been to love and be loved by each of you. You live in this world with such exuberance and grace. Thank you.

And finally, Lisa, my dear wife: I simply could not imagine living this life without you. You are my ally, advocate, lover, and best friend. You have been the face of God to me, and I am truly grateful for the journey we have been on together. Thank you.

Notes

Chapter 1

1. The past stories that have shaped our way of being in the world are central to understanding and loving our spouses. Heather MacIntosh writes, "While partners may have heard the title of the story of the traumas their partners have experienced, many do not know the story itself: the flesh and bones of their partner's most terrifying and vulnerable experiences." (Heather B. MacIntosh, *Developmental Couple Therapy for Complex Trauma: A Manual for Therapists* [London: Routledge, 2019], 169.)

In another study, MacIntosh found that spouses of sexually abused women knew only a cursory amount of information about the past abuse. Often the spouse did not know the age, context, or nature of the abuse, and the result was a lack of care and empathy regarding that portion of their story. (H. B. MacIntosh and S. M. Johnson, "Emotionally Focused Therapy for Couples and Childhood Sexual Abuse Survivors," *Journal of Marital and Family Therapy* 34, no. 3 [2008], 298–315, https://doi.org/10.1111/j.1752–0606.2008.00074.x.)

To know the past is to enter the stories that have shaped our brokenness and beauty. To do so requires the ability to be affected by what our spouses have suffered and a growing capacity to see how our failure of love has replicated and reenacted some of the harm of their past. This requires humility and openness to do the work of excavating our own past to make it safer for our spouses to enter the debris of their own past trauma. The remainder of this book will be an invitation to enter your own stories and the stories of your spouse. (See Dan B. Allender, *To Be*

Told [Colorado Springs: WaterBrook, 2005] and *Healing the Wounded Heart* [Grand Rapids: Baker, 2016]).

Chapter 2

1. Berit Brogaard, in a brilliant *Salon* article excerpted from her book *On Romantic Love: Simple Truths about a Complex Emotion* (Oxford University Press, 2015), states that falling in love is comparable to using cocaine. This is not a metaphor; it is a neurological reality. The brain produces adrenaline, oxytocin, and dopamine in the early stages of romantic love in a fashion indistinguishable from the use of cocaine. I view this as a gift from God to help us step over the threshold of risk and enter more deeply into a relationship that holds the complexity of being known. However, this period doesn't last forever. The rush of new love often lasts for less than eight months and sets us up for the good work of growing romantic love into a deeper *eros* called *agape*. Many couples have a nostalgia about the early days that fails to understand that this "high-love" period is not a bait and switch, but the opportunity to develop an even deeper and more lasting love. (Berit Brogaard, "Love Is Like Cocaine: The Remarkable, Terrifying Neuroscience of Romance," *Salon.com*, February 14, 2015, https://www.salon.com/2015/02/14/love_is_like _cocaine_the_remarkable_terrifying_neuroscience_of_romance/.)

Chapter 3

1. One study showed a correlation between deficits in emotional intelligence and lowered marital satisfaction with already present or high abandonment schemas. (P. O'Connor et al., "Can Deficits in Emotional Intelligence Explain the Negative Relationship Between Abandonment Schema and Marital Quality?" *Family Relations* 67, no. 4 [2018]: 510–522.)

Chronic emotional abandonment is traumatic for children, and often leads them to identify with the aggressor—in order to hold on to their needed attachment to their parents, they feel, think, and do what their parents require; blame themselves for being abused and for their family's unhappiness; and feel ashamed. (J. Frankel, "Treating the Sequelae of Chronic Childhood Emotional Abandonment," *Journal of Clinical Psychology* 80, no. 4 [February 2023]: 809–823, https://doi.org/10.1002 /jclp.23490.)

Chapter 4

1. The basis of this claim is found in Genesis 1:26–28, or what is often called the cultural mandate. We are made in the image of God. No other creature, from a hippopotamus to the archangel Michael, bears that designation. We are fearfully and wonderfully made (Psalm 139:14). Our Creator has endowed us with the capacity to multiply and rule. This is concrete language that implies fecundity and power. We are to be in and make families; we are to tend to and care for the earth. To multiply and rule is to intimately know one another—delight and labor together to explore and shape the earth into even greater glory and honor. The summary of this claim is that we are the face of God on behalf of one another.

Chapter 5

1. *Merriam-Webster*, s.v. "attune," accessed June 5, 2024, https://www.merriam -webster.com/dictionary/attune.
2. Edward Tronick and colleagues first presented the Still Face Experiment to colleagues at the biennial meeting of the Society for Research in Child Development in 1975. See Maria Robinson, *Understanding Behaviour and Development in Early Childhood: A Guide to Theory and Practice* (London: Routledge, 2011), 48.
3. J. Bowlby, *Attachment and Loss: Volume II. Separation, Anxiety, and Loss* (New York: Basic Books, 1973), 203.

Chapter 6

1. The brain response occurs in a process that is so complex that, though we can describe it, we can do so only in the most elementary terms. One neuroscientist describes the process as comparable to knowing something is happening in the state of Georgia that seems to be affecting something else in Nebraska. We can only look down from a vast distance and surmise how one process on the continent influences something on the other. Brain complexity might sound discouraging, but we know more about the brain and trauma today than we did five years ago. We will know more a year after you finish reading this section.
2. DMZs, or emotional demilitarized zones, are diabolic entrapments in a false sense of safety. Once an area of conflict is off-limits and isolated

from engagement, the fear and resentment attached to the original harm doesn't go away—it simply grows darker and develops stronger roots. The initial benefit of forming a DMZ is the relief that the conflict has disappeared and there is little discomfort. But like an unaddressed lump, it will likely metastasize. Not only is the problem going to grow, but it also will divide and develop into greater isolation and loneliness. We all know that you can be with someone or a group and feel lonely. Loneliness comes from having no one to witness and hold your suffering with honor and care. A DMZ leads to isolation and division not only in the relationship but in the body as well. Research shows that loneliness is tied to a host of complex physical ailments. (J. S. House, K. R. Landis, and D. Umberson, "Social Relationships and Health," *Science* 24 [1988]: 540–545.)

3. We actually don't even know how genetics shape learning or how learning experiences shape our DNA. We know it is never one or the other, and both shape aspects of our being.

4. As simple as this may appear, it requires a deep commitment to be part of the healing of the other. Equally, it requires allowing your spouse to be part of your healing. Researcher and theorist Sue Johnson reports, "When spouses were included in treatment for anxiety, success rates jumped from 46% to 82%." (Susan M. Johnson, *Emotionally Focused Couple Therapy with Trauma Survivors: Strengthening Attachment Bonds* [New York: Guilford Press, 2002], 4.)

    The assumption is as simple as this: if you are not part of addressing the struggles of your spouse, you are part of the problem. This is a radical shift in therapeutic understanding that used to see personal issues in one's life as unrelated to marriage in either cause or treatment. We are relational beings that are healed in relationship.

5. It is impossible to pause in the height of the biochemical stress response unless we are attuned to our bodies. Our normal heart rate is usually between 70 to 90 beats per minute, with women slightly lower and men higher. When our heart rate rises above 100, we are at the beginning stage of being emotionally hijacked. We must read our bodies with awareness of our default stress response and begin practicing emotional regulation. For victims of past trauma like sexual abuse, the hippocampus, the part of our brains that regulates our emotions, is often 8 to 15 percent smaller than those who have not suffered that harm. (Louis Cozolino, *The*

Neuroscience of Psychotherapy: Healing the Social Brain [New York: W. W. Norton, 2010], 266.)

Chapter 7

1. Curt Thompson, *The Soul of Shame: Retelling the Stories We Believe About Ourselves* (Downers Grove: IVP, 2015), 24.
2. Brené Brown, *Atlas of the Heart: Mapping Meaningful Connection and the Language of Human Experience* (New York: Random House, 2021), 137.
3. Online Etymology Dictionary, s.v. "shame," etymnonline.com, accessed May 1, 2024, https://www.etymonline.com/word/shame#:~:text=Old%20 English%20scamu%2C%20sceomu%20%22painful,Norse%20sk%C3%B6 mm%2C%20Swedish%20skam%2C%20Old.
4. Joshua Radin "You Got Me Thinking," in *Here, Right Now*, 2019.
5. Thompson, *The Soul of Shame*, 31.
6. Ann Voskamp, "Devotion 21: Unashamed Brokenness," in *The Way of Abundance: A 60-Day Journey into a Deeply Meaningful Life* (Grand Rapids: Zondervan, 2018), 93–96.
7. Brené Brown, *Daring Greatly: How the Courage to Be Vulnerable Transforms the Way We Live, Love, Parent, and Lead* (New York: Avery, 2012), 75.

Chapter 8

1. Contempt is the number one killer of intimacy and hope in a relationship. The research done on contempt by John and Julie Gottman is staggering. In their assessment of couples in the middle of conflict, they noticed four attributes that signaled the relationship would not last another five years: criticism, contempt, stonewalling, and defensiveness. (John Gottman and Robert Levenson, "The Timing of Divorce: Predicting When a Couple Will Divorce over a 14-Year Period," *Journal of Marriage and Family* 62, no. 3 [August 2000]: 737–745, http://doi.org/10.1111/j.1741–3737.2000.00737.x.)

Perhaps as amazing, Gottman's research discovered that the first three minutes of an argument can predict the quality and longevity of a marriage six years later. (John Gottman, Janice Driver, and Amber Tabares, "Repair During Marital Conflict in Newlyweds: How Couples Move from Attack-Defend to Collaboration," *Journal of Family Therapy* 26, no. 2 [June 2015]: 85–108, https://doi.org/10.1080/08975353.2015.1038962.)

The level of accuracy of prediction is so high that it exceeds any other measure by a country mile. This implies that how we address contempt in oneself and in one's marriage is one of the biggest factors in growing a marriage. A failure to engage and disrupt contempt is allowing cancer to grow without any treatment. As the research indicates, we need to be aware that in the first 180 seconds of a conflict we set the tone not only for that fight but also for what is ahead for years.

The good news is the hippocampus is capable of growing larger and gaining greater capacity to regulate emotions by engaging with the traumatic memories with greater compassion and grounding.

Chapter 9
1. Amanda Seitz, "Loneliness Poses Risks as Deadly as Smoking: Surgeon General," *AP News*, May 2, 2023, https://apnews.com/article/surgeon -general-loneliness-334450f7bb5a77e88d8085b178340e19.
2. Thompson, *The Soul of Shame*, 138.

Chapter 10
1. Barbara Brown Taylor, *An Altar in the World: A Geography of Faith* (New York: HarperCollins, 2010), 117–118.

Chapter 11
1. John Gottman, *7 Principles of Making Marriage Work* (New York: Harmony Books, 1999), 138.
2. Ted L. Huston, "What's Love Got to Do With It? Why Some Marriages Succeed and Others Fail," *Personal Relationships* 16, (2009): 301–327, https://doi.org/10.1111/j.1475-6811.2009.01225.x.
3. Robert Waldinger and Marc Schultz, *The Good Life: Lessons from the World's Longest Scientific Study of Happiness* (New York: Simon and Schuster, 2023), 171.
4. Pete Walker, "The 4 Fs: A Trauma Typology in Complex PTSD," Pete-Walker.com, accessed May 1, 2024, https://pete-walker.com/fourFs _TraumaTypologyComplexPTSD.htm.
5. Quoted in Lawrence Cunningham, *Francis of Assisi: Performing the Gospel Life* (Grand Rapids: Eerdmans, 2004), 146.
6. The discerning reader will note that the verb *forgive* is not part of the

process. It is not that we don't think forgiveness is central and crucial. We forgive as we have been forgiven. Jesus stated it with even greater clarity: "Whoever has been forgiven little loves little" (Luke 7:47). The complexity in using the word *forgive* is the vast misconception of what that process looks like. For many, it is a single act that forgets the harm and moves on. In fact, it is a process that relinquishes our right to revenge and seeks goodness for the other. (See Dan B. Allender and Tremper Longman, *Bold Love* [Colorado Springs: NavPress, 1992]).

The process of forgiveness is best understood as what we have called *repairing rupture*.

7. Kelly Richman-Abdou, "Kintsugi: The Centuries-Old Art of Repairing Broken Pottery with Gold," *My Modern Met*, March 5, 2022, https://my modernmet.com/kintsugi-kintsukuroi/.

Chapter 12

1. Christian Keysers and Valeria Gazzola, "Hebbian Learning and Predictive Mirror Neurons for Actions, Sensations and Emotions," Philosophical Transactions of the Royal Society of London, *Series B, Biological Sciences* 369 (1644), April 28, 2014, doi: 10.1098/rstb.2013.0175; Lea Winerman, "Mirror Neurons: The Mind's Mirror," *Monitor* 36, no. 9 (October 2005): 48.

2. Debbie Durand, "Exploring Increased Empathy to Enhance Wellbeing in Intimate Relationships," California Southern University ProQuest Dissertations Publishing, 2022. 29328197.

3. Donal Hebb, a well-known neurologist, said: "Neurons that fire together, wire together." This statement is called a Hebbian law.

Chapter 13

1. Stuart Brown, *Play: How it Shapes the Brain, Opens the Imagination, and Invigorates the Soul* (New York: Avery, 2009), 6.

2. Eugene Peterson, *Tell It Slant: A Conversation on the Language of Jesus in His Stories and Prayers* (Grand Rapids: Eerdmans, 2008), 69–70.

3. Myra Goodman, "Puzzling Out Play," *Spirituality & Health* 24, no. 2 (February 2021): 78–79, https://www.spiritualityhealth.com/articles/2021/02/20/puzzling-out-play.

4. Brown, *Play*, 218.

5. G. K. Chesterton, *Orthodoxy*, rev. ed.; repr. (Peabody, MA: Hendrickson, 2006), 55.

Chapter 15

Harrison Scott Key, *How to Stay Married: The Most Insane LoveStory Ever Told* (New York: Avid Reader Press, 2023), 295–296.

About the Authors

Dr. Dan B. Allender is a counseling psychologist whose therapeutic practice has been focused on marriage, trauma, and sexual abuse for more than forty-seven years. After receiving his MDiv from Westminster Theological Seminary, Dan earned his PhD in counseling psychology from Michigan State University. He previously served on faculty at the Biblical Counseling Department of Grace Theological Seminary (1983–1989) and at Colorado Christian University (1989–1997).

Dan is a pioneer of a unique and innovative approach to trauma and abuse therapy. In 1997, he and a cadre of others founded the Seattle School of Theology and Psychology, where he served as president from 2002 to 2009. In 2011, Dan, along with his wife, Becky, and Cathy Loerzel, founded the Allender Center to cultivate healing and train leaders and mental health professionals to courageously engage others' stories of harm. Dan is the author of numerous books, including *Redeeming Heartache*, *The Wounded Heart*, and *To Be Told*, and continues to serve as professor of counseling psychology at the Seattle School.

Dan and Becky have been married for forty-eight years and have three adult children and six grandchildren. They love hiking, fly-fishing, and sailing with good friends.

ABOUT THE AUTHORS

Dr. Steve Call is a clinical psychologist with more than twenty-five years of experience specializing in marriage counseling. He received his MA in Theology from Fuller Seminary, his MS in Marriage and Family Therapy from Seattle Pacific University, and his PhD in Clinical Psychology from Seattle Pacific University.

Steve and his wife, Lisa, are the founders of the Reconnect Institute, which offers resources, insights, and tools for cultivating meaningful connection in marriages. He is the author of *Reconnect* and an associate professor of counseling at the Seattle School of Theology and Psychology.

Steve and Lisa have been married for more than thirty-five years and have three adult children and three grandchildren. Steve enjoys playing on their farm, taking long walks on the beach of the Oregon coast, and fly-fishing in remote rivers in Montana.

RECONNECT INSTITUTE

"Story is the context for how we are known by our spouse."

Dr. Steve Call

The Reconnect Institute invites couples to courageously explore relational patterns that disrupt connection in their marriage while offering resources, insights, and tools to grow in greater intimacy. We help you experience more profound levels of awareness and understanding of yourself and one another, leading to a renewed connection in your marriage.

——

Offerings:
- Marriage Story Intensives
- Couples Intensives
- Story Groups

"

Marriage is meant for honor and delight.

"

thereconnectinstitute.com
Dr. Steve and Lisa Call

Allender Center
AT THE SEATTLE SCHOOL

Marriage is a meeting of two profoundly different stories.

We each carry core stories from our past—stories that have shaped us in ways we might not even realize. Stories of disappointment and desire, of hurt and hope. These stories impact how we show up in the present, especially in our closest relationships.

At the Allender Center, we invite you and your spouse to continue to explore your stories together. Through our marriage courses, conferences, and retreats, you can move toward greater understanding, honor, and delight in your relationship.

> "You must understand the *past* if you want to change the *present*."
>
> - Dr. Dan Allender

Start your journey today at:
theallendercenter.org/marriage

The Allender Center exists to foster healing and transformation in individuals, couples, and communities by helping them tell their stories with awareness and integrity. Founded in 2011 as part of The Seattle School of Theology & Psychology, we are committed to boldly addressing trauma and abuse, offering healing and training professionals to enter stories with care and courage.

Discover more resources, programs, and trainings at *theallendercenter.org*